The Pearl of Christian Comfort

Petrus Dathenus

Translated by Arie W. Blok
Introduced by Joel R. Beeke

Reformation Heritage Books
Grand Rapids, Michigan

The Pearl of Christian Comfort
© 1997 by Reformation Heritage Books

Reformation Heritage Books
3070 29th St. SE
Grand Rapids, MI 49512
616-977-0889
orders@heritagebooks.org
www.heritagebooks.org

Original hardcover edition 1997
First paperback edition 2005

Printed in the United States of America
21 22 23 24 25 26/12 11 10 9 8 7 6 5 4 3

ISBN 978-1-892777-42-3

For additional Reformed literature, request a free book list from Reformation Heritage Books at the above regular or email address.

"Therefore being justified by faith, we have peace
with God through our Lord Jesus Christ."
— Romans 5:1

"For Christ is the end of the law for righteousness
to everyone who believes."
— Romans 10:4

"Come unto me, all ye that labour and are heavy laden,
and I will give you rest. Take my yoke upon you,
and learn of me; for I am meek and lowly in heart:
and ye shall find rest unto your souls."
— Matthew 11:28-29

Introduction

Petrus Dathenus deserves more than an obscure foot-note on the pages of history. He was certainly the greatest among the early leaders of the Protestant Reformation in the Low Countries, and may justly be called the "John Knox" of The Netherlands.

Dathenus was born in 1531 or 1532 in Cassel, a town in Flanders, now part of Belgium. At an early age, he entered a Carmelite monastery near Ypres. There he studied medicine and the healing arts, knowledge which he would put to good use in later years. More importantly, among the Carmelites Dathenus met many who were in sympathy with the Reformation. When three monks who had embraced the Reformation were burned to death openly nearby, their heroic martyrdom and open confession of the Reformed faith moved many deeply. Dathenus had much opportunity to discuss these matters and the great evangelical truths of the Reformation. It pleased God to use these means to convert him to the Reformed faith as Dathenus came to know and experience that justification is by grace alone, through faith alone, in Christ alone.

By mid-century, Roman Catholic authorities became aware that the monasteries housed a growing number of sympathizers with the Protestant cause. A systematic search of the monasteries was launched as part of the Inquisition. Those cloisters found to be harboring Protestant sympathizers were dismantled, and many monks were burned alive in an effort to quench the Reformation movement.

At eighteen years of age, Dathenus fled the monastery, becoming a fugitive for the faith. To avoid death at the hands of the Church of Rome, he went to London where many refugees from the Lowlands resided. The young God-fearing king, Edward VI, supported the Reformation cause in England. Dathenus obtained work as a printer and attended the church of the refugees, learning much from the renowned Polish Reformer, John à Lasco (1499-1560), who was at that time superintendent of this congregation. By the early 1550s the congregation had more than four thousand members; services were conducted in both French and Dutch.

Under the leadership of à Lasco and another Reformer, Jan Utenhove (1520-1565), work began on an order of worship, a Reformed liturgy, and a metrical version of the Psalms for the large London refugee congregation. Another leader, Martinus Micronius (1522-1559), began work on a church order, entitled *Christian Ordinances*. As Dathenus began to assist these men he soon felt called to the ministry himself. Before long, both the leadership and the congregation were persuaded of Dathenus's abilities and in confirmation of his own sense of calling encouraged him to study theology full-time. He spent the years 1551 through 1553 in quiet, productive study, which would serve him well in the stormy trials of the years that followed. During this time he also married a former nun, Benedicta, with whom he had one child, Christiana.

In 1553 Edward VI died; Mary Tudor, called "bloody Mary" because of her violent persecution of Protestants in England, ascended the throne. The London church was scattered. The unfinished work of liturgy and church order went with a number of the Dutch refugees, including à Lasco, to Frankfurt, Germany, which rapidly became home to hundreds of Reformed refugees. Under à Lasco's guidance, the Frankfurt congregation extended a ministerial call to Dathenus, which he accepted. At the age of twenty-four, he was ordained into the ministry by Micronius in Frankfurt in September of 1555.

Again, peace did not last long. Alarmed by the growing Reformed presence, the Lutheran clergy of Frankfurt decided to require the Dutch Calvinist refugees to have their children baptized in the Lutheran church. Dathenus traveled to Geneva to speak with Calvin about this problem. Calvin advised Dathenus to submit to this requirement, but to affirm simultaneously Reformed convictions of the Lord's Supper. This solution worked only temporarily. By 1561 a radical Lutheran pastor, Joachim Westphal, goaded the Lutheran clergy and people to act against the Reformed congregation. On April 23, 1561 the Frankfurt government forbade the Reformed refugee congregation to worship any longer in their city, notwithstanding the plea of Frederick III, also known as Frederick "the Pious," who played such an important role in the composition of the Heidelberg Catechism.

Many of the Frankfurt refugees returned to England, where Elizabeth, who favored a more neutral stance on religious matters, had succeeded the staunchly Romish Mary. Others went back to the Lowlands and many were ultimately burned at the stake during the Inquisition. Sixty families, including Dathenus's, went to Frankenthal, a city located in the part of Germany known as the Palatinate, governed by Frederick III.

In Frankenthal Dathenus enjoyed productive and peaceful years (1562-1566) under Frederick III. He spent himself for the cause of the gospel and for the church of Christ. Soon after his arrival in the Palatinate he was called to serve as court pastor, which position he accepted in conjunction with pastoring the congregation of exiles.

Among other duties, he was moderator of several foreign congregations. He engaged in debate with Lutheran clergy on the ubiquity of Christ's body and became involved in political missions.

Dathenus's pen was also active in his Frankenthal ministry. He translated the Heidelberg Catechism into Dutch in 1563, the same year it was published in the Palatinate. On his recommendation, the Dutch churches adopted the Catechism as a creedal standard. He also published the Catechism together with his version of the metrical Psalms, which became known as the "Dathenus Psalms." Although he used the tunes and followed the text of the Genevan Psalter, the result was distinctly his own work. Hastily completed, Dathenus's version contained numerous imperfections. Nevertheless it became the Psalter of the Dutch Reformed Church and remained in use until the publication of the version of 1773. Dathenus's Psalter took hold of the hearts of the Dutch people, who recalled the days of persecution when the Psalms were sung at open-air meetings. They are used even today among Reformed Christians in certain parts of the Netherlands, and have been used by others who settled in North America.

Dathenus's third great contribution from the Frankenthal years was his role as father of the liturgy of the Reformed Churches. Drawing on a number of important Reformed sources, he compiled and edited the largest part of the liturgy as we know it today, in particular, the forms for the administration of Baptism and the Lord's Supper. He translated portions of the Palatinate liturgy used at Heidelberg, which in turn was based on Calvin's Genevan liturgy, modifying it in various places. He also used the work done at London by à Lasco and Utenhove. Dathenus's liturgy was first published in 1566 amid scenes of persecution, and in 1568 was adopted by the Convent of Wezel and prescribed for use in the churches. The traditional English version of these forms is a translation of Dathenus's liturgy in the classic formulation adopted by the Synod of Dort.

To Dathenus also we must attribute the order of service followed in conservative Reformed churches. So it is, whether we think of the Heidelberg Catechism, the use of the Psalter, or the liturgy and order of worship, the Reformed community of churches even today continues to enjoy the fruit of Dathenus's many labors at Frankenthal. May the Lord grant to us a heartfelt willingness to treasure this heritage of Word-centered, God-glorifying belief and worship for which our forebears labored, suffered, and died.

During his years in Germany, Dathenus's heart was still in the Lowlands and with his suffering Dutch brothers and sisters who were often put to death for espousing the Reformed faith. When in 1566 a compromise between the rulers of the Lowlands was ratified and afforded some hope of reprieve from persecution, he felt led to return to the Netherlands. It was not easy for him to leave Frankenthal where his work as pastor, court preacher, and liturgist had been richly blessed. The last twenty-two years of his life would be far less peaceable than his Frankenthal years.

Back in the Netherlands, Dathenus became a zealous, popular field preacher, condemning Rome and Spain vehemently and eloquently. He literally carried his pulpit on his back and preached wherever possible, sometimes to crowds that numbered from ten to fifteen thousand. Those were days when people were willing to walk many miles to hear the Word of God. He also held positions of leadership in the Dutch churches. In May 1566 he was elected president of the Synod of Antwerp; in 1568, he was elected president of the Convent of Wezel, held by the refugee churches in that German city. He was a delegate to the Synod of Emden in 1571 and president of the First National Synod of Dordrecht in 1578. Both these Dutch synods dealt with preparing a church order, a process to which Dathenus lent an important hand by adapting Micronius's work accomplished in London to the Netherlands situation. This process was not completed, however, until 1619 when the Church Order of Dort was formally ratified.

Meanwhile, Dathenus led a rather checkered life. His preaching soon brought him into difficulties, even with William of Orange, the leader in the fight against Spain. The prince wanted to grant Roman Catholics freedom of worship, but Dathenus strenuously opposed such a policy. When Dathenus began to incorporate strong political statements into his messages, emphasizing in particular that any concession made to Spain would eventually destroy the Reformed faith, William strongly opposed him. Consequently, after 1567 we find Dathenus back in the Palatinate for some years, where he pastored a congregation of Dutch, French, and Walloon exiles, and served as court preacher for John Casimir. In 1578 we meet him back in his homeland as a pastor in Ghent. He again began to travel, preaching extensively, also on political issues of the day. Due to his political involvement, William of Orange had him imprisoned for eight months and then sent him into exile.

Dathenus returned to Frankenthal as pastor, but nearly died from an epidemic disease. He was later dismissed by the congregation as he was no longer able to perform the work entrusted to him. Sadly, this dismissal, together with his rejection by William of Orange, deeply embittered him. He too was a man subject to like passions as we are (Jas. 5:17). He became a wanderer and took up the practice of medicine. According to his own testimony, he did not despise the Christian ministry but was forced into another occupation by his need to support himself and his wife. Wandering through Germany, he joined a revolutionary and heretical sect for a short time, which resulted in his being barred from the Dutch churches as well. Happily, the Dutch churches sent a delegation to lovingly convince him of his error. Upon their arrival, how grateful they must have been to hear from Dathenus's own mouth a confession of his sin and a declaration that he had parted from the sect prior to their arrival! Nevertheless, due to the infirmities of age and a life spent fleeing persecution, Dathenus was not able to return to the church or land that he loved. On March 17, 1588 he passed away in Germany, far from home and from his friends and church, but not far from the God whom he loved and served, and who washed away all his sins in the precious blood of Christ.

Somehow amid his many activities and trials, Dathenus also found time to write scores of letters. He wrote to many of the more renowned Reformers, but many of his letters have not been recovered. Calvin was one of his favorite correspondents. Another was Lady Elizabeth de Grave, to whom he wrote extensively in 1584 about soul-matters. These letters, written in the form of a dialogue, were collected and published forty years later, in 1624. They were entitled *De Paarl der Christelijke Vertroosting* (*The Pearl of Christian Comfort*) and are here presented in English for the first time, having been translated by Dr. Arie W. Blok with assistance from Bartel Elshout. Two editions of this work were used for the present translation, one published in Sneek, the Netherlands, in 1884, the other in Holland, Michigan in 1910. Both are based on a 1624 edition published in the Hague by Anthony Janz.

A dialogue between two or more persons was a fairly common literary genre among the Dutch for religious material that was intended to be instructive. The "pearl" Dathenus refers to is assurance of salvation and its accompanying peace of conscience before God. He refers to this as a "pearl," since in the folklore of his day, pearls were to be esteemed far above diamonds.

The Pearl of Christian Comfort is written as a dialogue between "Dathenus" and "Elizabeth." "Elizabeth" represents Lady Elizabeth de Grave. This work is a presentation of the Biblical doctrine of justification by faith and contains numerous echoes of the Heidelberg Catechism. Written to be of help and comfort to those in spiritual distress, it is characterized by an evangelical-experimental tone which would become typical of the early period of the Dutch Second Reformation (*Nadere Reformatie*).

One helpful feature of this book is its great number of supporting Scripture references. The translator has included these references, except in rare cases in which they did not seem to apply. He has added Scripture references in a few cases where a reference to a cited text was lacking, corrected references where the printer made an error, and adjusted references in cases where the Dutch verse numbers differ from those in the English version (which applies especially to the Psalms). Long sentences and paragraphs have been shortened to make comprehension easier for the reader, but great care has been taken to leave the author's message intact.

We trust that these spiritual dialogues, written more than four centuries ago, may bring spiritual encouragement to many in ways Petrus Dathenus would never have imagined.

— Joel R. Beeke

The Author's Dedicatory Epistle to the Honorable, Virtuous Elizabeth De Grave

My dearly beloved sister, grace and mercy to you by Jesus Christ our Lord:

Noble and virtuous lady, my very beloved sister, and good friend, Holy Scripture, all church histories and daily experiences give abundant testimony that the children of God are subjected to many crosses and assaults in this world. Yet no external cross can be compared to the internal strife to which believers are constantly subjected when awakened to a sense of sin — when we taste the wrath of God through the curse of the law, and the prospect of an open hell robs us of all hope of grace and salvation, distancing us from the power of the Holy Spirit who enables us to pray and cry out to God. It is very difficult to explain such strife to those who have never experienced it. It is very difficult to persuade people in their strife and to move them to faith. Yet those who have experienced this and, in the deep hell of their forsakenness, have for a time been discouraged and half-despairing, but afterwards, by God's grace and the work of the Holy Spirit, have felt and tasted the certainty of their salvation in Christ, can speak of this in a vivid way. The Lord be praised that I also have tasted and borne my portion, and as I understand, you have also not been entirely free from this cross.

In the long time in which I have served and walked, I have counseled and reassured many people who were honest, pious, and of good conscience, who because of the sinfulness of their nature and temperament had almost perished in despair (for Satan labors to this end and goes about day and night as a roaring lion). Therefore, it has often been my intention to improve on the little tract *The Consolation of the Sick*,[1] by writing something shorter and more Biblical in content for broader instruction of troubled consciences. I wish to help those who lack an adequate understanding of the difference between the law and the gospel, i.e., those who feel themselves unable to accept the doctrine of justification of grace by faith. However, because of my frequent journeyings and other occasions which overtook me, I have long been unable to carry out my intention, to say nothing of all the problems of the churches which keep me more than busy. I have not had the time for thorough meditation to be able to make a competent and orderly composition.

However, being moved by the dialogue we had with each other, it caused me to work out this dialogue in the manner of a friendly conversation, insofar as my situation permitted, until a time when God the Lord will give me the rest and opportunity to describe and explain these teachings in a broader, plainer, and more thorough way for the comfort of all poor sinners.

In order that you might be helped in the meantime, may you be able to study this comforting dialogue to the peace of your conscience. I have written this to you as a sure evidence and glorious remembrance of our godly

---

[1] Since the days of Dathenus, Dutch Psalmbooks have included this *Consolation of the Sick* (*Ziekentroost*), written by Cornelius van Hille.

friendship and unity which we have in Christ through the hand of the Holy Spirit. I present this in the hope that God may use this small labor to your comfort and that of many others in a wonderful way until the Lord will provide you with something better.

I request of you that you will receive this in thankfulness, read it and be comforted by it. Remember me in your prayers, and according to my slender ability, I will heartily do the same for you in order that we, together with all of God's elect, may walk in true faith which works by love, persevering steadfastly until the end and afterwards may live forever in blessed glory.

With all my heart, I commend all of you to the protection of our omnipotent God.

Your sincere brother and friend,
PETRUS DATHENUS

Date of posthaste to Ghent, June 26, 1585

A Christian dialogue from God's Word for the instruction and consolation of all troubled hearts who are not properly able to distinguish between the law and the gospel — that is, between Moses and Christ — who are troubled in heart by the burden of their sins and fear of damnation.

The dialoguing persons are
DATHENUS AND ELIZABETH

DATHENUS: God greet you, Elizabeth, my dear sister. Where are you coming from that you are so sorrowful? One would almost become depressed just by looking at you.

ELIZABETH: I come from a worship service where I heard God's Word preached.

DATHENUS: But how can that be? David says that the law of the LORD, which is perfect, rejoices the heart (Ps. 19:8). What have you heard that has done the opposite and made you so troubled and depressed?

ELIZABETH: Yes, it is true; in that same psalm where we read that God's Word is sweeter than honey and the honeycomb, we also read that in keeping God's Word there is great reward. But I find in myself that I am very far from keeping God's law. In spite of the knowledge which the Lord has given me, I am making the gulf of sin deeper, in that I daily make my sin-debt greater and bring myself deeper under God's curse and wrath. For it is written, "Cursed be he that confirmeth not all the words of this law to do them" (Deut. 27:26). To this our minister added that the servant who knew his Lord's will but did not do it would be beaten with double stripes (Luke 12:24). This has effectively admonished me and I find myself one of these servants. Therefore, do not I have good reason to be sad and to mourn?

DATHENUS: Everyone must acknowledge their shortcomings (Rom. 7:23) and have regret in their hearts, but they also must be mindful not to be overwhelmed with excessive sorrow (2 Cor. 2:7) — the kind that works death.

It seems to me that your sorrow is such a sorrow, and arises out of a great misunderstanding, which is that you do not distinguish between the law and the gospel because you do not rightly know the Lord Jesus. Therefore you are still far from a childlike fear. But perfect love drives out fear, for fear brings anguish, and one who fears in this way is not perfect in love. So please, dear Elizabeth, learn to understand God's Word better, so that you do not regard Jesus as another Moses. By this I mean, that you will not treat our Advocate and Savior as an accuser and condemner, which is the greatest dishonor with which people can dishonor Jesus.

ELIZABETH: I feel and bewail my ignorance and inadequacy enough, and I have found, as you say, that God's love in me is very incomplete. Yet I plead with you, dear brother, if you love my salvation, please be willing to take the time to instruct and comfort me, for I sincerely hunger and thirst after righteousness.

DATHENUS: This I owe to you and I am willing to do, but let us sit here along the bank of this watercourse under the green trees, where we are away from the noise of the crowd. Let us sit where the little birds laud and praise their Maker with happy songs. They will encourage us to delight in God and thank Him for all His benefits.

ELIZABETH: That suggestion pleases me. See, here is a pleasantly quiet and suitable place. Let us sit down here and speak frankly with each other. Just as Mary, Martha's sister, sat down at the feet of Jesus (Luke 10:39), setting aside all of her concerns, to hear His words, so will I seat myself here, being assured that you will explain that same Word of truth to me purely and faithfully by the Holy Spirit (Eph. 1:13; Col. 1:5).

DATHENUS: Mary chose the better part, which was that she took God's Word to heart. That is of all things most needful, although Martha did not give this a high enough priority (Luke 10:41). By taking God's Word to heart, you will also choose the better part which shall never be taken away.

Yet, since we cannot deal competently nor fruitfully with God's Word without His Spirit and grace, we will first call upon Christ with sincere prayer (Eph. 6:19).

ELIZABETH: You are very right about that. Please lead us in prayer and I will follow your words with an attentive heart.

DATHENUS: O Lord Jesus Christ, Thou hast promised Thy presence and grace to all those who are gathered in Thy Name, even when there are only two or three (Mat. 18:2). Therefore we pray Thee, that Thy Holy Spirit may be with us and in us (Luke 24:5). As Thou didst illuminate the hearts and minds of the apostles to understand Thy Word, so also enlighten our hearts and minds as Lydia's heart was prepared by Thy Spirit to receive and understand the words spoken by Paul (Acts 16:14), Thy chosen vessel. In the same manner, also open the ears of Thy maid-servant to hear and understand well what Thy unworthy servant will bring forth out of Thy Word, so that our conversation may be to Thy glory and to our comfort and salvation through Jesus Christ our Lord (1 Cor. 10:31).

ELIZABETH: Amen. Amen. Let it be so.

DATHENUS: Now, dear Elizabeth, what book is it that you have with you?

ELIZABETH: It is the Bible, or Old and New Testament, in a small format, with small print.

DATHENUS: That is as it should be. We have the Word of God, the sword of the Spirit, by which the Holy Spirit gives us the shield of faith by which we can quench the fiery darts of the devil (Eph. 6:16-17).

Elizabeth, open your heart to me and tell me about all that has troubled and burdened your heart (Matt. 9:16). Be assured, that our Savior Jesus Christ came to heal the sick. He will not break the bruised reed, nor quench the smoking flax. On the contrary, He has promised to give rest to those who come to Him with weary and heavy laden hearts (Mat. 11:28). He will strengthen and comfort you so that you will not only have a happy and quiet conscience yourself, but will also be able to comfort and refresh others.

ELIZABETH: The good God give and grant me that; just as I often pray with David, "Purge me with hyssop, and I shall be clean; wash me, and I shall be whiter than snow. Make me to hear joy and gladness; that the bones which thou hast broken may rejoice. Hide thy face from my sins. and blot out all mine iniquities.... Cast me not away from thy presence; and take not thy Holy Spirit from me. Restore unto me the joy of thy salvation; and uphold me with thy free spirit" (Ps. 51:7-12).

DATHENUS: That is a good and godly prayer; be assured that God has heard this prayer (John 16:23).

ELIZABETH: I still cannot feel that joy and gladness, nor

the free spirit. Neither do I feel the assurance of salvation in my heart, but I always feel myself beset with fears and doubts.

DATHENUS: That is no wonder, for a person's life on earth is an enduring struggle (Job 7:1); and just as the Spirit of God works to strengthen us in the true faith and reliance of the heart, without which no one can please God (Heb. 6:1), so also Satan is diligently attempting to keep us in doubt. He knows that a person who doubts is like the waves of the sea that are driven hither and thither by the wind. Therefore such a person will not receive the things prayed for, because such a person is unstable in all his ways (James 1:6-8).

Yet meanwhile, it is profitable, even essential, that we endure such assaults and the depths of despair[1] lest we become too elated (1 Cor. 12:7). Rather than exalting ourselves, we should humble ourselves under the mighty hand of God (1 Pet. 5:6), and pray without ceasing, so that we may have sympathy with those likewise afflicted.

But tell me, what is it that especially causes you to be so troubled and afflicted?

ELIZABETH: Oh brother, the reasons are heavy and many. First of all, I feel that I am one of those who knows God's will but does not do it (Luke 12:47). Therefore I can only expect to be afflicted with many stripes. After all, the Bible says plainly that all those who have sinned under the law will be judged by the law; for not those who hear the law but those who do the law will be justified (Rom. 2:12-13). Also Christ

---

[1] Dathenus says "cast into the depths of hell," but since people of his day often spoke of hell metaphorically, when they really meant *despair*, a literal translation here might confuse the modern reader.

demands of us "If you love me, keep my command-ments" (John 14:15). He also says, "Every branch in me that beareth not fruit he taketh away" (John 15:2). Such branches wither away and men gather them and they are burned (John 15:6).

John the Baptist testifies the same where he says, "And now also the axe is laid unto the root of the trees: every tree therefore which bringeth not forth good fruit is hewn down, and cast into the fire" (Luke 3:9). I do not find good fruit in me, but on the contrary, whenever God performs anything good by His Spirit in my heart, it is defiled by the effects of my evil nature. Besides that, I feel daily more iniquities within me than I have hair on my head (Ps. 40:12). Therefore I often complain, "O wretched man that I am! who shall deliver me from the body of this death?" (Rom. 7:24).

Are these not reasons enough to be sad and de-spondent?

DATHENUS: Yes, indeed, but I say again, that the great-est cause of your troubles is because you are so despon-dent and feel yourself under condemnation,[2] wounded unto death, and laden with many burdens. You do not rightly know Him who can deliver you, heal you and remove your burdens; and He will if you will only go to Him. Your problem is that you are still ignorant of the first principles of the Christian religion.

Therefore, with you I must begin with the funda-mentals. So tell me, my dear sister, do you know how God's Word must be divided in order to speak of it wisely and with proper discrimination?

---

[2] Here again, Dathenus says, "in the depths of hell," when he is speaking of a sense of being condemned.

ELIZABETH: Yes, indeed, for God's Word is divided into the Old and New Testaments, or in the doctrines of the prophets and the apostles (Eph. 2:20).

DATHENUS: That distinction is not adequate to divide God's Word rightly (2 Tim. 2:15), as Paul expresses it, or to adequately explain it. John declares that the law came by Moses, but grace and truth came by Jesus Christ (John 1:17).[3] Here John distinguishes between the ministry of Moses and the ministry of Jesus Christ. In order to show a clear distinction, the apostle refers to Moses as a servant but Christ he calls the Son, Lord and heir (Heb. 1:2; 3:5-6). A still stronger distinction is made when the apostle calls the ministry of Moses a ministry of the letter that kills and condemns, but calls the ministry of Christ a ministry of the Spirit and of righteousness (2 Cor. 3:6).

However, in order to stay with more common distinctions and more useful expressions, we say that God's ministry is divided into the distinct parts of law and gospel.

ELIZABETH: Such is also my understanding.

DATHENUS: But what do you understand by the word "law"?

ELIZABETH: I hold the law to be all that Moses has commanded, but especially that which is contained in the two tables of the law, also all that is further taught in the Old Testament.

DATHENUS: Oh Elizabeth, you are still quite far from a right understanding of the truth! Is it your opinion then, that the Old Testament saints had no gospel at all?

---

[3] Dathenus attributes these words of the apostle John to John the Baptist.

ELIZABETH: That is how I have always understood this to be.

DATHENUS: Then it is easy to understand why, until now, you have been so despondent and discouraged.

ELIZABETH: Then how must I understand this matter of the law and the gospel, in order to come to a proper understanding of God's Word?

DATHENUS: I will explain it to you in a simple way. The law is a declaration of the unchangeable will of God. By the threat of eternal damnation it binds everyone to complete and perpetual obedience, to fulfill all that God has commanded in His commandments (Deut. 5:6; 27:26). Wherever either the Old or New Testament teaches that this perfect obedience is required of us, there the law is emphasized and taught (James 2:10; Gal. 3:12).

ELIZABETH: But do you find such a teaching anywhere in the New Testament?

DATHENUS: Really quite often. This teaching is laid upon us in the Bible verses that you have just quoted, in which you expressed how deeply you have been saddened and afflicted. All precepts that admonish us and exhort us to perform all that we owe to God and to our neighbor are *law*. For example, the entire fifth chapter of Matthew, where Jesus says to us, "But I say unto you, That whosoever is angry with his brother without a cause;...whosoever shall say, Thou fool" (Mat. 5:22); "whosoever looketh on a woman to lust" (Mat. 5:28); and all similar statements — they are all the *law*, which demands of us that which we are not able to keep and requires what we are not able to perform. Just to cite another example, where Jesus says, "If thou wilt enter into life, keep the commandments." (Mat. 19:17). There He speaks of and prods us with the law; also wherever He requires something similar of us. So also for various reasons Paul, Peter, John, and other apostles have done, in their writings and exhortations.

ELIZABETH: Explain to me, please, why Christ who came, not to condemn us but to save us, would so strongly emphasize to us the demands of the law? Also why would His apostles have done the same thing?

DATHENUS: You must come to know and correctly comprehend when and why the law was given and what purpose the law serves even today. Then your eyes will be opened and you will receive lasting comfort. At the same time, you will also understand how and in what ways God has powerfully and so graciously saved us from the power and condemnation of the law by Jesus Christ.

ELIZABETH: Please explain it thoroughly to me.

DATHENUS: First of all, you should realize that the law did not have its beginning when Moses received the two tables which were inscribed by the finger of God, and later explained in his five books. The law had its beginning when God created Adam in His image and implanted His law in Adam's heart. The law of God was there then, as the image of God in which Adam was created, made as Paul says, in true righteousness and holiness.

ELIZABETH: I have never looked that deeply into that. Still, I have to acknowledge that what you say is true. For Adam was created to rightly know and love his Creator, to obey Him and to do good to his neighbor in love.

DATHENUS: You are right in the way you see it. The

whole law consists of love toward God and our neighbor, as the whole of Scripture teaches. Yet beyond that,
we must also know that God not only gave Adam His
law but also the ability and liberty to completely fulfill
the law. For Adam, as he was created, was wise, pure,
and immortal. Once Adam had fallen from innocence,
he became a servant and slave of sin and of the devil.
Adam stood before the choice of life and death, and
by the exercise of his own free will, he chose death.
By this fall Adam not only brought death to himself,
but also to all his descendants.

ELIZABETH: But how could Adam rob his descendants
of the holiness, wisdom, and free will in which he had
been created, when they had not yet even been born?

DATHENUS: That is not difficult to understand. Adam
did not have children until after his fall, when he was
made subject to sin and damnation and had lost the
image of God, which consisted in true holiness and
righteousness. That is why the Bible tells us that Adam
begot a son in his likeness (Gen. 5:3). Just as a man
who has been sold into slavery cannot beget children
who are freer than himself, so also Adam could not beget
children that were less fallen than he himself was.

ELIZABETH: Please explain it better to me with an illustration and testimony of Scripture, because it seems
to me important to understand this thoroughly.

DATHENUS: That is certainly true. Notice how the apostle teaches that Levi, being still in the loins of his
grandfather Abraham, gave a tithe, because Abraham
gave tithes to Melchizedek (Heb. 7:9).

So also, we have all sinned when we were still in
the loins of our ancestor Adam. That is why Paul
declares that death came upon all people through one

man, in whom they all have sinned (Rom. 5:12). He goes on to say that through one man's offense, the judgment was upon everyone to condemnation.

Elsewhere Paul says, "we...were by nature the children of wrath, even as others" (Eph. 2:3). That agrees with what Christ teaches us when He says, "That which is born of the flesh is flesh" (John 3:6). How can anything be clearer than that?

God testified to this already before the great flood, complaining that people were not willing that His Spirit would reprove them "for he also is flesh" (Gen. 6:3).

ELIZABETH: These testimonies are certainly very clear; but what does the LORD mean when He says that humans are flesh?

DATHENUS: He means that humans are fleshly minded, blind and ignorant in things concerning God (1 Cor. 2:14), disinclined to real virtue and inclined toward all that is evil. This is what God Himself declares when He says that "every imagination of the thoughts of his heart was only evil continually" (Gen. 6:5).

That is also why Paul states that the wisdom or mind of the flesh is death (Rom. 8:6). Elsewhere he tells us that the natural man does not understand the things of God because they are foolishness to him (1 Cor. 2:14). That is the reason that Paul labels us not only as children of wrath by nature, but adds that we are dead through our trespasses. Yes, he even says that we are without hope and without God in the world (Eph. 2:3-4, 12).

By this we are informed that just as a dead person cannot do the works of a living person, so also, someone who is spiritually dead cannot do the works which require that a person be spiritually alive.

ELIZABETH: Is it then your conclusion that a natural, unregenerated person, does not truly have a free will to do what is good?

DATHENUS: Yes, indeed, for how can a person have a free will to do good, when one has made oneself to be a bond servant of sin and of the devil (John 8:34)?

ELIZABETH: If that is so, then why did God give us His law, when He knew beforehand that we would not be able to keep it? Does God not seem to do us an injustice when He demands of us that which we are not able to be or to perform?

DATHENUS: I know that some would make the unchristian accusation against God of unfairness; yes, even of tyranny. Yet, by this they display an arrogant rashness, for who has ever prevailed in opposition to God? Whenever a person enters judgment with God, He will always maintain His cause (Job 9:12). Who shall say to Him, "What makest thou?" (Isa. 45:9; Rom. 9:20). Therefore we should always be content with what is God's will, as Christ is when He says, "I thank thee, O Father, Lord of heaven and earth, because thou hast hid these things from the wise and prudent, and hast revealed them unto babes. Even so, Father: for so it seemed good in thy sight" (Mat. 11:25-26).

Those who would accuse God thereby display their great ignorance. Notice that in creating humanity, God gave humans the freedom and ability to keep His law perfectly. How can it be unjust of God to require back from us what He has once granted us?

ELIZABETH: I will admit that it is true that humanity, in the first state before the fall, had that ability, but not any longer, as you yourself have stated. But does it not seem unjust to demand of someone that which he is no longer able to do?

DATHENUS: No, it is not unjust when the one who makes a demand only demands the exercise of an ability that the other has been given. I ask you, Elizabeth, was the king unjust when he demanded repayment of the ten thousand talents owed him (Mat. 18:24)? Did the debtor's inability to repay make the creditor's demand an unjust or unfair demand?

ELIZABETH: No, for he acknowledged the debt, and falling on his knees, pleaded for compassion and promised to repay the entire debt (Mat. 18:26).

DATHENUS: Yet it is written there, that the servant was unable to repay.

ELIZABETH: Yes, that is clearly stated.

DATHENUS: So therefore the king's demand was not unjust, for if you lend someone ten thousand talents out of the goodness of your heart, you are not unjust in strictly demanding repayment when your debtor has squandered your money and come to poverty.

ELIZABETH: Why would it be unjust if I made such a demand?

DATHENUS: Therefore God also does not act unjustly when He demands from us what He has given us in creating us, even though we are now not able to repay our debt!

ELIZABETH: I must admit that, as far as Adam is concerned. But why does God make that demand of us, when He knows very well that we, who have been ruined in Adam, are not able to meet His demand?

DATHENUS: First of all, to demonstrate His good right that He has upon us and to remind us of our just debt, so that we, with all our shortcomings, poverty, and inability (Mat. 11:28), might fall down before Him (Isa. 55:6), and fervently plead with Him for pardon (Heb. 4:16). And afterwards, by a wholehearted faith and confident trust, receive and appropriate Jesus Christ who took our debt upon Himself and completely re-paid it (Heb. 9:12). Yes, He even erased the record of legal demands that was against us, nailing it to His cross (Col. 2:14; Gal. 2:20; Luke 7:50).

ELIZABETH: Oh, what a wonderful comfort that is for my troubled and burdened conscience!

DATHENUS: Just as this is very comforting, so it also is certain and true. For this is what Paul is teaching us with these and similar words, namely, that "by the deeds of the law no flesh shall be justified in his sight: for by the law is the knowledge of sin" (Rom. 3:20). Also, "Nay, I had not known sin, but by the law: for I had not known lust, except the law had said, Thou shalt not covet" (Rom. 7:7; Exod. 20:17).

As summation, Paul points out that the law is our disciplinarian,[4] or that which leads us to Christ, to be justified by faith. However, once we have come to faith, we are no longer under the disciplinarian or guide.

ELIZABETH: That is comforting and true. But accommo-date yourself to my ignorance, and explain it to me even more.

DATHENUS: I will gladly do that. You did understand what we discussed earlier about the blindness, aliena-tion and depravity of the natural man, in which he is spiritually dead before God, did you not?

---

[4] Dathenus uses the term *dwangmeester*, which can be roughly translated as "slave-driver." His meaning is that the law, by its rigor, drives the believer to flee to Christ for refuge.

ELIZABETH: I did hear you say that, but I did not understand it very well.

DATHENUS: In spite of what the real state of man is before God, he likes to see himself as being pious, holy, and righteous. This we can see by the example of the rich young ruler who boasted that he had kept all the commandments of God from his youth (Mat. 19:20). When the penitent woman who was a sinner touched Jesus, Simon the Pharisee regarded himself as if he were not likewise a sinner (Luke 7:39). Another example is the Pharisee who thanked God that he was not a sinner, as the poor publican (Luke 18:11).

ELIZABETH: Indeed, that is the case all too often with unbelievers.

DATHENUS: Oh Elizabeth, God grant that it does not happen with those who think themselves to be the best of Christians, who see the splinter in another's eye, but do not notice the beam in their own eye.

ELIZABETH: But can this also happen with those who truly know God?

DATHENUS: Alas, yes, far too often. I have to complain that I come across it many times, and I do not doubt that you sometimes have discovered it in yourself. Spiritual pride, self-love and self-centeredness have not died in the children of God. You can see this very plainly in the example of Laodicea, where they saw themselves as rich and enriched and having lack of nothing. But the Lord testifies to the contrary, that they were poor, miserable, blind and naked (Rev. 3:17).

ELIZABETH: That, indeed, is true.

DATHENUS: Because we are so blinded by spiritual pride that we do not feel our miserable state, the law of God serves as an eye salve (Rev. 3:11), to clear up our dim vision, and as a mirror (James 2:5), in which we can see and acknowledge how far we fall short. He does this in order that we will be displeased with ourselves (Ps. 19:13) and become ashamed like the poor publican who did not even dare to lift up his eyes to heaven, and say with him, "God be merciful to me a sinner" (Luke 18:13).

ELIZABETH: I also need that eye salve and that mirror.

DATHENUS: Not only you, dear Elizabeth, but also the holiest of people. Therefore also the more experienced of God's elect see themselves mirrored faithfully when they have made a sincere confession (Ps. 19:13; 38:5; Job 13:23; 14:4; Isa. 38:17; 64:6; 1 John 1:9).

The highest perfection of people, as long as they live on earth, lies in a sincere confession of imperfections.

ELIZABETH: This cannot be denied, for who does not have to say and confess with David, "Who can understand his errors? cleanse thou me from secret faults" (Ps. 19:12)?

Please, also teach me something of the gospel which, as you taught me earlier, is the other part of God's Word. I now pretty well understand what the law is about.

DATHENUS: This I would wish you from the heart, but I fear that you still have quite a deficiency in the knowledge of the law; but we can always make up that deficiency later. So now let us talk about the gospel.

Tell me, Elizabeth, what definition would you give me of the gospel?

ELIZABETH: All that Christ and His apostles have taught us and handed down to us in writing in the New Testament.

DATHENUS: Here you are again making quite a big mistake. Have you forgotten so soon that which I pointed out earlier — that Christ and His apostles (Rom. 8:3) also proclaim and enforce the law? Don't you remember that they exhort all people to keep the commandments of God, which we are not able to do (Acts 15:10)?

ELIZABETH: Yes, that is true, but I had almost forgotten that. So please instruct me. What is the true gospel?

DATHENUS: The Greek word for *gospel* denotes joyful good news which causes people to speak and sing joyfully and be glad in heart, just like the good news that came to Israel that David had triumphed over the arrogant Goliath and slain him (1 Sam. 18:6).

Such also is the good news of the gospel that proclaims to us and tells us that God will be gracious to a poor sinner, and will forgive and forget our sins (Jer. 31:34; Heb. 8:12). Yes, for Christ's sake (1 Tim. 1:15) God will regard us as holy and righteous (2 Cor. 5:21), out of pure grace, by faith alone, without adding any works (1 Cor. 1:30; Rom. 3:28).

ELIZABETH: I thank you very much for showing me this contrast between the law and the gospel. Now I am beginning to understand what it is all about. But tell me, is the gospel also given in the Old Testament?

DATHENUS: Oh yes, and in overflowing abundance! As you know, Abel (Heb. 11:4), also Abraham and the other saints of the Old Testament, were justified through faith; yes, they saw the day of Christ with the eyes of faith (John 8:56).

ELIZABETH: Yes, that is true. That is why all believers are called children of Abraham (Gal. 3:7).

DATHENUS: Tell me, Elizabeth, what was the foundation or the ground on which Abraham's faith rested, and on which the faith of all children of God must rest?

ELIZABETH:Paul testifies that no one can lay any foundation other than the one that has been laid; that foundation is Jesus Christ (1 Cor. 3:11). For Jesus is the living stone, rejected of men (Ps. 118:22) but chosen of God and precious — as Peter tells us — on which foundation all believers must be built up as living stones (1 Pet. 2:4-5; Isa. 28:16).

DATHENUS: This is true and well said. From this it follows that Abraham's faith was also founded on Christ. Abraham knew and saw Christ (John 8:56) by faith in the promises (Gen. 12:8), as God said to him, "in thy seed shall all the nations of the earth be blessed" (Gen. 22:18). The LORD further explains this with "and all the nations of the earth shall be blessed in him" (Gen. 18:18). Paul tells us that Christ is this seed (Gal. 3:16). Therefore, Abraham had the true gospel of Christ, of which the main point was that Christ has delivered him and all believers from the curse and condemnation (Deut. 27:26) that sin has brought upon the entire human race. Not only that, but Christ has blessed and given us eternal life. Was that not a joyous gospel and good tidings to Abraham?

ELIZABETH: Yes, there is no doubt about that!

DATHENUS: From this you can understand that the first promise made to Adam in Paradise, that the seed of the woman would crush the head of the serpent (Gen. 3:15) was also the genuine gospel. Abel was justified by faith (Heb. 11:4), which focuses on Jesus, while never having received a word of promise except those words about the seed of the woman. Therefore it is affirmed beyond contradiction that Christ was proclaimed in this promise, and that therefore this same promise is the fundamental premise of the gospel.

ELIZABETH: Yes, that necessarily follows, for the word of Christ is and always remains true: "I am the way, the truth and the life: no man cometh unto the Father, but by me" (John 14:6).

DATHENUS: You understand that correctly. Abel, Noah, and others could have eternal life through no other than Jesus Christ (John 14:6; John 10:7; Isa. 6:6). Just as the aforementioned promises were truly evangelical promises, so there are also countless other such promises found in the prophets (Isa. 42:1-4; 51:4-5; 61:1; Jer. 23:6; Dan. 9:26 and Psalms 2, 40, 72, 100, 132).

There are also all the sacrifices of Abel, Noah, and Abraham and the priesthood of Melchizedek; yes, also the entire Levitical priesthood, with all its sacrifices, burnt offerings and purifications. They are all evangelical symbols and proclamations of the deliverance and salvation that was to come to pass by Christ's sacrifice in the fullness of time (1 Cor. 10:1-5), as the whole epistle to the Hebrews explains (Heb. 8:5). Christ also confirms this, saying, "And as Moses lifted up the serpent in the wilderness, even so must the Son of man be lifted up: that whosoever believeth in him should not perish but have eternal life" (John 3:14-15).

ELIZABETH: God be praised and believed, who has privileged me to hear and understand this! Now I realize that this is the same message that Christ, when raised from the dead, explained to the disciples from Moses, the Psalms, and the prophets (Luke 24:27, 44). That is why He opened heart and mind to understand the Scriptures of the Old Testament; for, as He witnesses elsewhere, they testify of Him (John 5:39).

DATHENUS: I thank God for having brought you this far, and I do not doubt that He will lead you further, until you, like Paul, will come to comprehend what is the length and breadth and depth and height of the most excellent love of Christ that surpasses knowledge (Eph. 3:18). But to strengthen my case, I might add that Paul testifies that God promised this gospel beforehand through His prophets in the holy Scriptures (Rom. 1:2).

Peter confirms this, saying that the Spirit of Christ, which was in the prophets made careful search and indicated these times, first, by the suffering of Christ, and secondly, by the glory of Christ that would follow (1 Pet. 1:10-12). Since this is so, do they not greatly err who reject the Old Testament, which is the foundation of the gospel, as no longer useful, and would deprive us of it?

ELIZABETH: They truly do err, for Christ is the cornerstone, upon which not only the apostles have built, but also the prophets (Eph. 3:20).

Also Paul clearly testifies that he has not spoken nor taught anything except what Moses and the prophets have said.

But now, dear brother, please tell me, what purpose will this ability to distinguish between the law and the gospel serve?

DATHENUS: It will serve to comfort and strengthen you by faith in Jesus Christ, and by the aforementioned gospel promises, quiet and overcome the anxiety of your conscience which is troubled by the killing letter of the law (2 Cor. 3:7).

You heard, as you mentioned before, that the servant who knew his lord's will and did not do it, shall receive a severe beating (Luke 12:47). That means that on the one hand, those who keep the law will be righteous, but on the other hand your sins are more than the hairs of your head (Ps. 51:5) — and what other legal pronouncements and threats there are besides — you shall not let these and similar reasons disturb you nor discourage you, but they will serve you as a schoolmaster to bring you to Christ (Gal. 3:24), to seek Him by faith (Rom. 10:8, 12), to find Him and to appropriate all that the law can possibly demand and all that you need to be saved.

ELIZABETH: I will do that by God's grace (1 Cor. 1:30). Yet faith must be followed by good works (Gal. 2:20) or faith is dead, just as James says. Therefore he also teaches that Abraham was justified by works when he offered his son Isaac (James 2:20). In the same way we must also follow him in good works.

John agrees with this, saying: "Whosoever abideth in him sinneth not: whosoever sinneth hath not seen him, neither known him...let no man deceive you: he that doeth righteousness is righteous, even as he is righteous" (1 John 3:6-7).

Christ teaches the same, saying that the vine that does not bear fruit is thrown away, withers and is burned with fire (John 15:6).

These and similar admonitions that demand obligated duties and gratitude make me uneasy and troubled, since I find myself very weak in these things.

DATHENUS: There is no doubt that we must always strive for childlike gratitude (Mat. 5:16), not to be partly or entirely justified through it, but to show by it that we have already been justified by grace through faith (2 Pet. 1:8). Therefore, dear Elizabeth, I was right when I said earlier that you are still defective in the matter of understanding the law and how we are delivered and freed from it.

ELIZABETH: I will admit that we are freed from the law as far as the ceremonies are concerned (Col. 2:16); but where adhering to and keeping the ten commandments is concerned, you admit, do you not, that we are bound to it all the days of our lives (Rom. 13:9)?

DATHENUS: Yes, Elizabeth, I heartily acknowledge that. Yet, please, let us deal with this material in an orderly way; then God's Word will inform and satisfy you.

You said earlier that faith without works is dead. This does not contradict Paul who testifies that, "in Jesus Christ neither circumcision availeth any thing, nor uncircumcision; but faith which worketh by love" (Gal. 5:6). In this, to keep it short, we are in agreement; but regarding the matter of good works, you will, I hope, admit the following things: First, good works must not be done to gain merits or reward, for hirelings shall not be heirs but will be shut out. Secondly, the good works that God requires and that are described as such in God's Word, must be done out of childlike love and out of faith. All that is done without faith is sin, even if they are in themselves the holiest and most excellent deeds that ever were performed.

ELIZABETH: That cannot be denied.

DATHENUS: That is what Paul affirms, when he says: "For ye have not received the spirit of bondage again to fear; but ye have received the Spirit of adoption" (Rom. 8:15). As I told you earlier, so John also testifies, "There is no fear in love" (1 John 4:18). Therefore Paul calls for love that comes from a pure heart, a good conscience, and sincere faith (1 Tim. 1:5).

Besides that, we have to admit that good works are never, as far as we are concerned, holy, pure, and perfect before God. We must confess with the prophet that we have all become like one who is unclean, and all our righteous deeds are like filthy rags (Isa. 64:6). That is why Christ also says, "when ye shall have done all those things which are commanded you, say, We are unprofitable servants: we have done that which was our duty to do" (Luke 17:10). We cannot boast of any merits anymore than a person can who has only paid what he owed. For that reason Paul refers to us as debtors (Rom. 8:12).

ELIZABETH: Oh yes, I admit that. Yes, I often lament that my good works are so imperfect and that I have not paid my just debts of duty and gratitude toward God and my neighbor.

DATHENUS: All godly people must deplore this as long as they live, because to be frank about it, instead of paying off something on this debt we make our guilt-debt greater each day. Therefore, we should always pray with David, "enter not into judgment with thy servant, for in thy sight shall no man living be justified" (Ps. 143:2). Finally, when it comes to good works, you admit that as far as they are good, they are really not our works, but God's work in us, who is at work in us both in the willing and the performing (Phil. 2:13).

ELIZABETH: That is exactly how I feel about it, for we are not competent in ourselves to do anything really good. So Christ very rightly declared, "...without me ye can do nothing" (John 15:5). Therefore I confess that God, out of pure grace, crowns and rewards in us His own works. As the prophet says, "for thou also hast wrought all our works in us" (Isa. 26:12).

DATHENUS: That is truly and well said. Yet tell me
further, Elizabeth, how do you understand the words
of James when he says that Abraham was justified by
works (James 2:21)? For Moses claims that God regarded Abraham as righteous long before he had received his son Isaac (Gen. 15:6). Paul teaches us the
opposite [of James], namely, that Abraham was not
justified by works, but by faith (Gal. 3:6). Therefore he
has nothing to boast of before God (Rom. 4:2-3).

You have also earlier acknowledged David's testimony to be true when he says that no one living shall
be righteous before God (Ps. 143:2), seeing how (as
Moses writes in Exodus 34:7), that no one is guiltless
before God (Rom. 3:20). How then was Abraham justified by works?

ELIZABETH: You must be right; yet the epistle of James
was also written through the Holy Spirit's inspira-
tion,[5] which cannot be contradictory. Please, I beg you,
dear brother, teach me how I should understand this.

DATHENUS: It is to be understood that the Holy Spirit
does not contradict Himself. Therefore both that
which Paul writes and what James writes must be
true. However, you should understand that faith and
the word *justified* are used and understood in the Bible
in different ways. Sometimes *faith* is used to indicate
a merely superficial, historical or cursory knowledge
or opinion, which not only godly people possess, but
even the devils have (James 2:19). Such a faith will not
make people righteous nor blessed.

There is also a justification before the eyes of men,
as when Paul says that he was, as to righteousness

---

[5] Here Dathenus reads "written by the Holy Spirit."

under the law, blameless (Phil. 3:6). That is what James speaks of as justification (James 2:21).

The true denotation and definition of faith is that whereof Jesus speaks, "He who believes in the Son has everlasting life" (John 3:36). This faith is not only a knowledge and perception, but also a hearty trust, which the Holy Spirit brings about in the hearts of the elect children of God, whereby they firmly trust and are assured that their sins are forgiven them, and true righteousness and eternal salvation are given to them out of grace (Ps. 2:11) — and that without the addition of works, only for the sake of Christ's merits[6] (1 John 2:2; Heb. 13:20; 10:10, 14).

Paul is talking about this kind of faith, and of a righteousness that is valid before God (Eph. 2:8; Phil. 3:9). Therefore Paul and James are not really contradicting each other.

ELIZABETH: I thank you sincerely, dear brother and friend. With this explanation you have brought peace and serenity to my heart. Now please continue to verify that which you began to explain earlier.

DATHENUS: I will do just that, and for that reason I want to ask whether you think that the apostle John contradicts himself?

ELIZABETH: No, not in any way.

DATHENUS: You have quoted John earlier, where he declares that which indeed is true, that he who abides in Christ does not sin (1 John 3:6). On the one hand,

---

[6] This is another "echo" of the Heidelberg Catechism. M. Borduin says, "The tone of our Catechism can be discerned in this entire book, but especially here. Here we are given almost the complete answer to Question 21, 'What is true faith?'" *Paarl der Christelijke Vertroosting*, ed. by M. Borduin (Holland, MI: H. Holkeboer, 1910), p. 43.

John says, "He that committeth sin is of the devil" (1 John 3:8). On the other hand, John had said earlier, "If we say that we have no sin, we deceive ourselves, and the truth is not in us. If we confess our sins, he is faithful and just to forgive us our sins, and to cleanse us from all unrighteousness" (1 John 1:8-9). He also says, "And if any man sin, we have an advocate with the Father, Jesus Christ the righteous: And he is the propitiation for our sins: and not for ours only, but also for the sins of the whole world" (1 John 2:1-2).

But doesn't it seem that these pronouncements contradict each other? Doesn't he also say, "If we say that we have not sinned, we make him a liar, and his word is not in us" (1 John 1:10)?

ELIZABETH: It does seem as if John is inconsistent and contradicts himself, yet I am sure that this cannot be. So please explain to me just how I should understand these words.

DATHENUS: James says that we all offend in many things (James 3:2); and again: "Confess your faults one to another, and pray one for another" (James 5:16). Peter exhorts his readers: "Above all things have fervent charity among yourselves: for charity shall cover the multitude of sins" (1 Pet. 4:8). If all are of the devil who sin, then how can there be anyone who can really pray, "Forgive us our sins" (Luke 11:4)? How can anyone who is of the devil call upon God, or be capable of real prayer? What must we think of the prayers of the holiest children of God who have sinned, when they pray to God and are forgiven? We see this not only in the prodigal son (Luke 15:16) and the publican (Luke 11:13) — that they prayed when they were laden with sins, and their prayers were heard —

but also that David was certainly a most vile sinner; yet God heard him when he prayed, "For thy name's sake, O LORD, pardon my iniquity, for it is great" (Ps. 25:11). Moreover, there are a multitude of similar examples.

ELIZABETH: I know that is true, for as the sick person desires medicine because of sickness, so also do we desire the grace of God through Jesus Christ because we are miserable sinners. Yet the words of John, "He that committeth sin is of the devil" (1 John 3:8), must also be true.

DATHENUS: Seeing that John does not intend to contradict other Scripture nor himself, we should let John be the interpreter of his own words. John also writes in this same epistle; "If any man see his brother sin a sin which is not unto death, he shall ask, and he shall give him life for them that sin not unto death. There is a sin unto death: I do not say that he shall pray for it. All unrighteousness is sin: and there is a sin not unto death. We know that whosoever is born of God sinneth not" (1 John 5:16-18).

Notice, on the one hand, the distinction here between sins that do not lead to death — which also can be committed by those who are brothers or sisters, about which we may and should pray, so that they may receive life — and, on the other hand, those sins that lead to death, about which we are told that we should not pray. Such sins are sins of complete apostasy from God and revealed truth; of blasphemy and persecution of the truth (Heb. 6:4-6): the apostasy which is called the sin against the Holy Spirit (Mat. 12:31; Mark 3:28-29). All who willingly sin these sins are of the devil (John 8:44), for thus the devil has sinned from the beginning; namely, a constant aggression against God who created him so gloriously and arrayed him so magnificently.

Those who are born of God, that is, those who are united to Christ by the Spirit of adoption (Rom. 8:15), do not sin. They do not commit the sin of apostasy, for no one shall pluck Christ's sheep out of His hand (John 10:28). It is impossible for God's elect to be deceived or permanently led astray.

Therefore, though the children of God, against their will, are beset and burdened by the remnants of sin as long as they are in the flesh, and though these are still sins, they are not sins unto death. Having been washed by Jesus, we still need a daily washing of our feet. The good branches which bear good fruit the Father purifies more and more, so that they may bear more fruit (John 15:2).

That is why the apostle, lamenting that with his mind he serves the law of God but with his flesh he serves the law of sin (Rom. 7:25), still comes to the conclusion that there is no condemnation for those who are in Christ Jesus, who do not walk after the flesh but after the Spirit (Rom. 8:1, 5).

Here the apostle teaches us two precious things: First, that our flesh serving the law of sin (if with our minds we serve the law of God), does not damn the elect believer; secondly, that those who do not walk according to the flesh, serve God — yes, even though their flesh, against their will, serves the law of sin; that is, even though they still remain subject to their remaining sin and their corrupt nature.

The flesh wars against the spirit and the spirit against the flesh, so that they do what they do not want to do. They are still to a degree captive, and therefore it is not they that do it but sin which dwelleth in them.

ELIZABETH: O dear brother, how these words of John

have often oppressed me, yes wounded me nigh unto death! Now you have relieved and refreshed my heart by explaining them so thoroughly with John's own words and other pronouncements of Scripture. Now I understand, praise God, the difference between sins that lead to death (1 John 5:16-17) and sins that do not lead to death.

Indeed, it has to be as you say, or even the holiest people would be of the devil; for we all remain besmirched with sin as long as we live here on earth.

DATHENUS: That is sure and evident. Cannot we see clearly how serious the accusation against Peter was, because after he had received the Holy Spirit and preached for many years, he acted so hypocritically in Galatia that even Barnabas was led astray (Gal. 2:11-14)? That is why Paul withstood and rebuked Peter publicly.

But this does not mean that Peter instantly became of the devil, as some would apply John's words (1 John 3:8) from similar cases. This was in Peter an uneradicated fault that God did not count against him.

This is also what Paul teaches: "Brethren, if a man be overtaken in a fault, . . . restore such an one in the spirit of meekness; considering thyself, lest thou also be tempted" (Gal. 6:1).

ELIZABETH: This example of Peter clarifies and strengthens what you are saying so beautifully. This harmful hypocrisy in Peter, after he had received the Holy Spirit, was not a minor transgression, seeing that Barnabas who had been a faithful fellow worker with Paul for so long had been led astray by it, and others were also offended or led into error by it.

Remember what Jesus says: "But whoso shall offend one of these little ones which believe in me, it were better for him that a millstone were hanged about his neck, and that he were drowned in the depth of the sea" (Mat. 18:6).

But please continue your instruction.

DATHENUS: Yes, Peter would have been in deep trouble if God had wanted to enter into judgment with him. Yet we must not ignore that Christ also emphasized the requirements of the law, as we saw earlier.

I must also add here a short explanation of the words of John the Baptist, when he speaks of trees that do not bear good fruit (Mat. 3:10), and also the words of Christ, when He speaks of removing the branches in Him that do not bear fruit (John 15:2).

ELIZABETH: O yes, please do that now, before it slips your mind, for these and other statements have often troubled me.

DATHENUS: This is not a difficult matter. John and Christ are not speaking of trees or branches that bear some fruit or only a little fruit, but of those that bear no fruit at all.

Who is there among the children of God, those that have been grafted into Christ (Rom. 11:17), who does not produce by grace some fruit at times? Christ praised the widow as one who did very well, who only gave two mites. He also says that the giving of a cup of cold water will not go unrewarded (Mat. 10:42). Have you not read that Christ praises fields that produce only thirtyfold as much as a field that produces a hundredfold (Mat. 13:8)? Christ praises the servant who had received two talents and gained two more talents as much as the servant who had received five talents and gained five more (Mat. 25:19-22).

On the one hand, it is one thing to produce no fruit

at all, as we read of the fig tree that produced nothing except green leaves and a beautiful appearance (Matt. 21:19); and, on the other hand, quite another thing to bear some fruit, according to the measure of the gifts that each has received (Rom. 12:3; Eph. 4:7).

In the construction of the tabernacle of the LORD, the poor people who donated goat skins or hair were as welcome to God as those who donated gold, silver or gems (Exod. 25:22-24). So it still is now.

ELIZABETH: O brother, hearing that makes me feel that I have become another person, through happiness and spiritual joy by the Holy Spirit. Yet, please do not forget your declared intention to further explain to me the law and its characteristics, insofar as you consider it necessary for my instruction.

DATHENUS: I will do that with God's help. Have you forgotten what you said earlier, Elizabeth, that we are free from the works of the law as far as the Old Testament rites are concerned; but that we are still bound to complete obedience to the ten commandments as long as we are in this life?

ELIZABETH: Yes, I did say that, and I still maintain that we owe God complete obedience to the ten commandments, and that for two reasons:

First, because in the beginning, God created us according to His image (Gen. 1:26); secondly, because He redeemed and gave us salvation by grace (Eph. 2:8), through Jesus Christ when we were lost and condemned sinners (Rom. 5:8).

DATHENUS: You are correct in saying that we have this obligation as long as we live. But tell me frankly, Elizabeth, is it your view that anyone here in this life can keep God's commandments perfectly?

ELIZABETH: It does seem that one can do that with the help of the Holy Spirit, for Christ tells us that His yoke is easy and His burden is light (Mat. 11:30). Also, John says, "For this is the love of God that we keep his commandments; and his commandments are not grievous" (1 John 5:3). That is why Paul says, "I can do all things through Christ which strengtheneth me" (Phil. 4:13).

DATHENUS: Oh Elizabeth, here you have again gone very far astray. On the one hand, it is true that Christ's yoke is pleasant and His burden is light (Mat. 11:30), because Christ requires nothing of us except faith and love (1 John 4:21), for which He gives us His Holy Spirit (Luke 11:13).

On the other hand, Christ teaches us to pray without ceasing for the forgiveness of our sins (Luke 11:4); John also testifies that if we say that we have no sin, then the truth is not in us (1 John 1:8).

The Holy Scriptures show us often enough that there is in us no perfect righteousness that can stand before God (Isa. 64:6), even though there is in us a principle of a new life and holiness. Else we would not need the death of Christ, for as Paul points out, if righteousness could be by the law, then Christ died needlessly (Gal. 2:21). God accepts our first steps and partial compliance as complete righteousness, because His children have received Christ by faith, in whom they find and appropriate for themselves the perfection that is acceptable before God.

In this framework, Christ declares His disciples to be sanctified, even though there remained many imperfections in them — not only small imperfections, but some of them quite evident and gross, as also soon became apparent. Nevertheless, they were sanctified in truth, not in themselves but in Jesus Christ. So Jesus asserts when He says that they were not of this world, even though worldly affections still dominated them too much (John 17:14).

So Paul also refers to believers in general as "called to be saints" (1 Cor. 1:2), "God's elect" (Rom. 8:33), the "sanctified" (1 Cor. 6:11), even though they still had many shortcomings and sins, as his epistles and exhortation amply testify. Also, Zacharias is said to be blameless and righteous in the eyes of God, and yet he was soon afterwards struck dumb because of his unbelief (Luke 1:6, 20).

Because God does not count against His children the sins which they have committed (Rom. 4:8), but rather imputes to them, out of grace, the holiness and righteousness of Christ, which they have not done, therefore God regards them as having kept His commandments, even though there is in them only a small beginning of the holiness which God demands of them in His Word.

When Paul says that he can do all things (Phil. 4:13), he is not contradicting himself; he is simply saying that by God's grace he can endure both prosperity and poverty. When it comes to keeping the commandments of God, he confesses, "I know that in me (that is, in my flesh,) dwelleth no good thing" (Rom. 7:18); in fact, that entire chapter confirms that. Therefore he also says very clearly that God has done in Christ what the law could not do (Rom. 8:3).

ELIZABETH: That is firm and true, and oh, how poor I am; as far as I myself am concerned, I have to admit and bewail that all my doings and knowledge are faulty, and as you explained, all my righteousnesses are as filthy rags (Isa. 64:6). Therefore, let us not neglect to commit ourselves to our obligated duties to serve God in all perfection.

DATHENUS: It is very true, Elizabeth, that we are and remain debtors to the law. The question is, however, whether we can pay that debt ourselves, or whether another must make payment for us. Regarding our ability, Peter's testimony is unmistakable: "Now therefore why tempt ye God, to put a yoke upon the neck of the disciples, which neither our fathers nor we were able to bear? But we believe that through the grace of the Lord Jesus Christ we shall be saved, even as they" (Acts 15:10-11).

There Peter teaches that neither the holy patriarchs, nor they, the apostles, were able to keep the law; that is, in regard to the perfect keeping of the ten commandments, for the observance of the ceremonial precepts was a light matter. If righteousness were by the law (as claimed above), then Christ died needlessly (Gal. 2:21). However, true believers have in Christ all that the law can require of them. That is why Christ is called the end of the law for righteousness to everyone who believes (Rom. 10:4).

For even though the law requires perfect righteousness from believers, they refer the demanding law to Christ, in whom they have become the righteousness of God; that is, a righteousness that is acceptable to God (Col. 1:14). If the law demands that believers shall pay for their sins, they refer the law again to Christ who has so completely fulfilled all the demands of the law that He also blotted out the handwriting of ordinances that was against us, nailing it to His cross (Col. 2:14).

That is, He canceled them so that the law can no longer condemn us, no more than it can condemn Christ unto whom we are united, seeing that Christ has delivered us from the curse of the law (Gal. 3:13). Paul is therefore correct when he says, "O death, where is thy sting? O grave, where is thy victory? The sting of death is sin; and the strength of sin is the law. But thanks be to God, which giveth us the victory through our Lord Jesus Christ" (1 Cor. 15:55-57). This proves that in Christ we are not only set free from the strength of the law and of sin, but also from the power and dominion of death and hell.

From this proceeds the spiritual glorying and confidence of Paul, when he exclaims, "Who shall lay any thing to the charge of God's elect? It is God that justifieth. Who is he that condemneth?" (Rom. 8:33-34).

ELIZABETH: O my friend, these are such wonderful, true, and comforting teachings; they are almost beyond my understanding! So I beg you, please explain this truth to me in even clearer terms.

DATHENUS: I notice that you still cannot properly distinguish between Moses and Christ; you believe that Christ does not drive us to the ceremonies of the law as Moses did to his people. However, regarding the keeping of the ten commandments are concerned, you believe that Christ and Moses are alike.

ELIZABETH: Yes, that has for a long time been my view and understanding.

DATHENUS: But in this you are totally deceived (1 Cor. 3:9). The difference between Christ and Moses is as great as that between life and death. This is clearly demonstrated by the words of John: "For the law was given by Moses, but grace and truth came by Jesus

Christ" (John 1:17). Likewise we read, "For God sent not his Son into the world to condemn the world; but that the world through him might be saved" (John 3:17). Christ says therefore, "Do not think that I will accuse you to the Father: there is one that accuseth you, even Moses, in whom ye trust" (John 5:45).

Hereby Christ teaches that as much as the function of an accuser or prosecutor is distinct from that of a mediator, reconciler, or defender, so distinct is also Moses' function and office from that of Christ (Rom. 4:14-15). Moses can only bring to us a knowledge of sin, a sense of God's wrath, and the resulting uneasiness of conscience and fear of damnation. However, Christ takes away sin, along with the deserved punishment, brings peace and serenity to the conscience, and causes God's children to be cheerful and of good courage (Rom. 5:1) Christ *gives* to His own all that Moses *demands* from His own.

ELIZABETH: Oh, this ability to distinguish between Christ and Moses is so very necessary for all those who are burdened with the distressing and slavish fear of death and damnation; yet people find it so difficult to rightly grasp this distinction.

Dathenus, would you please explain more clearly this matter of Christian liberty, which we have in Christ from the condemning law of Moses, by way of some illustrations?

DATHENUS: I will gladly give my best efforts to achieve that end. The Holy Spirit has indeed explained this matter with several illustrations. First, we have the illustration of a minor child that is placed under his guardians. There seems little that distinguishes such a minor from a servant, even though the child is heir and owner of its property. Instead, the child is compelled to action and beaten by the guardians. The child must be obedient and subservient as long as he is under guardianship. Upon reaching maturity, however, he is now at liberty to use his property as he desires (Gal. 4:1-2).

So also it is with believers who, while under the law are always in bondage to fear and anxiety (Gal. 4:3), and being subject to a disciplinarian and guardian (Gal. 3:24), are denied the use of the benefits and liberty which God has given them through Christ. But when they reach the age of manhood through faith in Jesus Christ who has delivered them from all bondage, then they are free — yes, sons and heirs through Jesus Christ (Gal. 3:4-7).

ELIZABETH: Truly, that is very beautiful and comforting. From which I understand, in short, that the law no longer has the power to accuse or condemn those who have come to Christ because of their sins, for which Christ has fully paid, anymore than a guardian who has been discharged from his domestic position may impose his will upon a young man who has reached maturity and whom the authorities have determined to be a free and independent man.

DATHENUS: Now you understand this matter correctly. Paul explains the same issue in detail with the allegory about Abraham's two sons — the one born to Abraham by Hagar according to the flesh, the other born to Sarah according to the promise. But the son of the bondwoman was cast out and was not permitted to be an heir with the son of the free woman (Gal. 4:22-24).

Likewise, all who seek righteousness by the law of the ten commandments are slaves and as it were Hagar's children; they will also not abide in the house to all eternity. Believers, however, who seek salvation in Christ by grace, are children of Sarah and are free — and therefore are also true heirs. This is indeed what Paul teaches, saying that the Gentiles who did not pursue righteousness attained righteousness, even the righteousness that is by faith. Israel did not attain righteousness, however, because they sought it through the law (Rom. 9:30-31).

ELIZABETH: This proves therefore that it is not of him that wills or runs, but of God that shows mercy (Rom. 9:18).

DATHENUS: That is certain. But the clearest and most beautiful illustration used to explain this matter comes to us from Paul, where he compares the believer to a woman and Moses to her first husband, and Christ as the second husband of this woman. Paul teaches that the woman is bound to her first husband as long as he lives, but as soon as he has died, she is free from the law of her first husband (Rom. 7:2), so that she then has the right and freedom to enter into marriage with another man (Rom. 7:3).

To all true believers who have appropriated Christ by faith to be their bridegroom and husband (2 Cor. 11:2), Moses has died and is completely dead. Therefore the apostle states clearly: "Wherefore, my brethren, ye also are become dead to the law by the body of Christ; that ye should be married to another, even to Him who is raised from the dead, that we should bring forth fruit unto God" (Rom. 7:4).

Tell me then, Elizabeth, why are you yet concerned about the law of the first husband who has died, now that you by faith and out of grace have married another husband — a husband who has personally assumed all your debt, and thereby paid it in full so that no debt remains whatsoever? Has He not made you a partaker of all His benefits, so that you may boast of and glory in them as being your own?

ELIZABETH: O, this is most wonderful indeed and comforting beyond measure to all troubled consciences, namely, to all those to whom God has given grace to understand this and to heartily believe it! Yet I find it somewhat difficult to grasp — and especially to rightly appropriate it to myself.

DATHENUS: No wonder. There are all too many who have been called to teach others and who still do not understand this as thoroughly as is indeed necessary. Pray to God for His grace, however, and diligently reflect upon what I have taught you from God's Word. To your comfort you will experience, taste, and perceive that this is the very truth indeed.

ELIZABETH: I am well assured that this is the truth, for you have held nothing else before me except God's pure and clear Word. I also hope that the Lord will cause me to feel and know this in His time.

DATHENUS: This I also sincerely hope for you; but don't forget, Elizabeth, how Paul, after telling us that by the works of the law no flesh shall be justified before God (Gal. 2:16), says with a confident heart: "For I through the law am dead to the law, that I might live unto God. I am crucified with Christ: nevertheless I live; yet not I, but Christ liveth in me: and the life which I now live in the flesh I live by the faith of the Son of God, who loved me, and gave himself for me. I do not frustrate the grace of God: for if righteousness come by the law, then Christ is dead in vain" (Gal. 2:19-21).

ELIZABETH: Those are indeed comforting words. Please give me a clearer and more extensive explanation of them.

DATHENUS: I will do that. First, the apostle says that he, through the law, died to the law (Gal. 2:19).

ELIZABETH: That is a very wondrous manner of speech: "For I, through the law, died to the law."

DATHENUS: Yes, this is indeed true, but as wondrous as it is, it is also full of comfort and precious instruction. You have heard the law referred to as our first husband who has passed away (Rom. 7:3), and that we are also dead to the law by the body of Christ; that is, by the essence and truth of all the shadows and figures comprehended in Christ. Therefore the law cannot lay claim against us, just as a husband who has died cannot exercise any dominion over his former wife.

Now, how such an alienation — yes, a dying process — comes to pass, Paul explains here when he says that "he, by the law, is dead to the law." The law does not profit me except that it brings me to a knowledge of sin (Rom. 3:20; 7:7), and holds the wrath of God (Rom. 4:15) and the curse (Deut. 27:36) before my eyes, without giving me any solace or hope of salvation or life (2 Cor. 3:6).

Thus I have completely died to the law and am alienated and divorced from the law (Gal. 2:19).

ELIZABETH: That is certain and true, for even the greatest of the saints in the world cannot expect from the law anything except deserved punishment for their sins, and damnation. Christ tells us that in the day of judgment we shall have to give an account of every careless word we have uttered (Mat. 12:36).

DATHENUS: That is evident, but the Lord forgives His

own as graciously as He deals strictly with them to humble them.

However, to continue the explanation of the above passages — the apostle adds, "that I might live unto God" (Gal. 2:19); hereby pointing out that a person cannot live unto God before one has sought life in God's grace — no, not before one has become dead to the law.

Those who live to the law, that is, they who still expect to obtain salvation by the works of the law, have never felt the strength of the law. They know nothing of death and condemnation to which they are subject, and therefore they are neither hungry nor thirsty for the righteousness of Christ (Mat. 5:6).

Therefore, they are before God as if they were dead — as the Pharisee who praised himself, trusted in himself, and condemned others (Luke 18:10-12). For God desires and welcomes contrite, troubled, and oppressed hearts who feel their poverty, destitution, and sickness (Mat. 9:20), in order that He might comfort, refresh, enrich, and heal them with the riches of His grace in Jesus Christ (Mat. 11:28).

Consider, for example, the rich young ruler who claimed to have kept all of God's commandments from his youth. He lived according to the law (Luke 18:18-24); therefore he was dead unto God. However, the woman who was a sinner and washed Christ's feet with her tears, received the grace of God in Christ through a steadfast faith and heartfelt trust. (Luke 7:37-50). She was dead to the law and therefore she lived unto God.

ELIZABETH: Thanks be unto God that by way of this analogy I begin to understand these things better, namely, that those who live to the law have not felt the condemning power of the law. They therefore seek and expect to receive life and salvation by the deeds of the law. Such people are dead to God. On the contrary, however, those who see in the law nothing but their sins, death, God's wrath, and their well-deserved condemnation, turn away from that same law and go to Jesus Christ and by faith in Him appropriate God's grace. They die to the law and live unto God because by confessing their insignificance, they yield to God's grace and appropriate it by faith.

DATHENUS: That is a correct understanding of this matter, for even Paul teaches us this when he says, "I am crucified with Christ" (Gal. 2:20); "Christ lives in me;" and "Christ gave himself for me" (1 Pet. 2:24). That is to say, I am one body with Christ (1 Cor. 1:30). Therefore, His suffering and death are my payment and my satisfaction, and His life in perfect holiness and righteousness is my life. For all that is His I also possess together with Him. It is for that reason that He died and surrendered Himself. He did not do so for Himself, but for me (John 17:19; Rom. 8:32), because He loved me (Rev. 1:5), as the Scripture also declares and teaches in a most comforting manner in other places (Eph. 5:25).

ELIZABETH: God be praised and thanked who has granted that I should hear and understand in some measure this very comforting and evangelical teaching. Now I also want to put away the first husband, that is, Moses, and die to him, cleaving only to my second husband, meaning Jesus, who loved me and gave Himself for me (Gal. 2:20).

DATHENUS: God give you the grace to do that. "Stand

fast therefore in the liberty wherewith Christ hath made us free, and be not entangled again with the yoke of bondage" (Gal. 5:1), or else Christ will be of no benefit to you (Gal. 5:2). Those whom the Son makes free are free indeed (John 8:36), and where the Spirit of the Lord is, there is liberty (2 Cor. 3:17).

"Who shall lay anything to the charge of God's elect? It is Christ that died, yea rather, that is risen again, who is even at the right hand of God, who also maketh intercession for us." Who can separate us from the love of God (Rom. 8:33-35)?

ELIZABETH: Yes, that is very true! If God is silent and satisfied — yes, even accounts us righteous for His Son's sake — who then has any reason to accuse us?

DATHENUS: No one — that is certain. But just as Balaam who, for love of filthy lucre, sought and desired to curse God's people and could not, but instead was compelled to bless them against his will, saying, "How shall I curse, whom God hath not cursed? or how shall I defy, whom the LORD hath not defied?" (Num. 23:8), so must all enemies also render righteous whom God Himself acknowledges and beholds as righteous (Rom. 8:33-34).

There is one accuser, cast down from heaven, who accuses us day and night (Rev. 12:10), but over against him we have Jesus Christ, the Mediator (1 Tim. 2:5) and our Advocate (1 John 2:1), who always lives to makes intercession for us (Heb. 7:23).

Since Christ, the highest Judge, prays for us, and the Father, out of grace, accounts us as righteous, who can cause any detriment to our salvation?

ELIZABETH: Truly, not one creature — particularly

since Christ, who is the righteousness of the Father, has made a complete satisfaction for us.

DATHENUS: He canceled out the record of guilt that was against us, nailing it to His cross (Col. 2:14); not a single debt remains. Therefore, the apostle speaks very much to the point when he declares that Christ, with a single sacrifice, has sanctified for all time those that are His (Heb. 10:14); that is, perfectly through the truth (John 17:19). God's children find as much comfort in God's righteousness as in His compassion. Since Christ has rendered full satisfaction to God, He, being righteous, cannot twice demand payment for their guilt — else He would be unrighteous. The completeness of Christ's payment is sufficiently proven by His resurrection on the third day. That would not have happened if there had still been any sin of His elect for which Christ had not made satisfactory payment.

Paul therefore says that Christ was delivered over to death for our offenses and was raised again for our justification (Rom. 4:25).

ELIZABETH: The canceling of the record of our debt of guilt is a clear evidence of Christ's payment in full (Col. 2:14). John therefore says that He is the atoning sacrifice not only for our sins, but also for the sins of the whole world (1 John 2:2). Oh, how comforting and worthy of recognition it is that believers can rejoice in God's righteousness as well as in His merciful compassion, whereas others quake and tremble as much as they rejoice in God's compassion!

DATHENUS: Indeed, it is comforting beyond measure, as well as glorious and full of comfort, that Paul says that God made Christ, who knew no sin, to be sin for us, so that we might become the righteousness of God in Him (2 Cor. 5:21).

Thus we are by the gracious imputation of the Father not only righteous, but righteousness itself, since we are one with Christ (John 17:21) who is Jehovah — that is, God in His true essence — our righteousness (Jer. 23:6), and the Sun of Righteousness (Mal. 4:2) who imparts to us His superabundant brilliance and beautiful radiance so gloriously (John 1:16-17).

In Christ, we are not merely given something, but we are given everything. Christ therefore says, "And the glory which thou gavest me, I have given to them: that they may be one, even as we are one" (John 17:22). This all comes forth from the bottomless fountain of divine love with which the Father has loved us (John 14:21; 16:27).

Could we imagine or wish for a greater or more complete love than the love with which the Father has loved His Son (John 15:9)?

ELIZABETH: Oh, the indescribable goodness and mercy of the Father! Who can fathom or adequately consider this love that has been shown to us poor sinners? Who would not be set aflame by such a burning love? Oh, how blessedly happy we are, Dathenus, on whom this grace has now been bestowed in the New Testament by Jesus Christ!

DATHENUS: Yes, we are blessed indeed, Elizabeth, for no tongue can express, no mind can even imagine (1 Cor. 2:9), the grace that God has bestowed on us in Christ when He made us — who were children of wrath (Eph. 2:3), ungodly, (Rom. 4:5) and enemies (Rom. 5:10; Eph. 2:12) — His beloved children and heirs, yes, fellow heirs with Christ of all His benefits (Rom. 8:16-17).

He has so assured us of this (1 Cor. 1:20-22; 5:5) that we cannot doubt, unless we want to accuse God of being a God who is untrue — yes, even perjurious.

In addition, such grace is not only given to us, but also to all believers of the Old Testament who have wholly entrusted their hearts to Christ.

ELIZABETH: Yes, that is also my understanding, for the children can receive no better inheritance than that which has been the Father's possession beforehand — although we now have a clearer and more complete knowledge and revelation of the grace of God than that which was given in the Old Testament, as you have previously shown me.

DATHENUS: You have retained this correctly and understood it well. That was the reason that Isaiah did not speak of Christ as one who would come after many years had passed, but he spoke and wrote by the Holy Spirit as of one who had already come and fulfilled all things (Isa. 53:3-17). Faith enabled him to see the salvation that was to come as if it were already present (Heb. 11:1).

Christ also declares that Abraham had seen His day and was glad (John 8:56). Paul testifies that the rock from which the children of Israel drank, was Christ, and that the forefathers have eaten of the same spiritual food as we (1 Cor. 10:2-4), and have drunk of the same spiritual drink. For the efficacy of the sacrifice of Christ, which took place at Jerusalem in the fullness of time, extends from the beginning of the world to the end, to save those who by true faith receive and appropriate Christ's sacrifice.

ELIZABETH: Oh Dathenus, now you have completely relieved my conscience from all that burdened it. Now I, as His child, can only complain that I cannot adequately show the gratitude to God that I should show Him for such benefits.

DATHENUS: We must exert ourselves with a confident faith (1 Tim. 1:15) and a joyous heart (Phil. 4:4), proceeding from faith and filial love — all this according to the gifts God has given us.

Yet we must also no longer torment ourselves about those things wherein we fall short due to weakness (Heb. 4:16; 2 Cor. 12:9), seeing that we have perfection in Christ (2 Cor. 5:21). Else we make of Christ another Moses and show that we have not received the spirit of adoption but the spirit of bondage again to fear (Rom. 8:15). Remember that John says, "Herein is our love made perfect, that we may have boldness in the day of judgment: because as he is, so are we in this world" (1 John 4:17).

Pay close attention to these words! Why should we not have boldness in the day of judgment, seeing that, dying in faith, we shall not go to perdition and be summoned to judgment, but pass from death unto life (John 5:24). For Christ who has been appointed as Judge in the last judgment (John 5:22), has fully paid for us and now is our Advocate (1 John 2:1), has also said, "Father, I desire that they also, whom thou hast given me may be with me where I am" (John 17:24). What reason do we have then to fear in any measure, seeing that the God who demands righteousness has accepted us as righteous, and that the Judge is our brother (Heb. 2:11), Redeemer (1 John 2:2; 1 Tim. 2:6), spokesman, and Advocate?

ELIZABETH: How can anyone think this through thoroughly and not be joyful and comforted by Paul's words, "For I am persuaded that neither death nor life, ... nor any other creature, shall be able to separate us from the love of God, which is in Christ Jesus our Lord" (Rom. 8:38-39)? My only complaint, as I said, is that I cannot manifest my gratitude as I should because I still find myself beset and laden with many sins.

DATHENUS: Elizabeth, this is something that you have in common with all of God's chosen children. Has there ever been anyone among those who have been received by God in grace and upon whom many precious gifts and benefits have been bestowed, that have not often fallen into grievous sins (Job 3:1; 25:4; Isa. 64:6)? God has nevertheless not held their sins against them, but has acknowledged them as His children. For our salvation is truly comprehended in this, that although we are beset and burdened with many sins (Prov. 20:9), they are not counted against us but freely forgiven (Ps. 32) — yes, God also totally forgets them (Jer. 31:34; Heb. 8:12).

ELIZABETH: This is all true, but when I truly examine my heart and feelings according to the rule of thankfulness, I find that even after having received the knowledge of the truth, I am still sinning frequently and grievously each day. Because of that I can hardly find assurance and true peace of heart.

DATHENUS: O Elizabeth, what do I hear you saying? It seems that you are unlearning everything and are regressing. You have just blessed and thanked God so joyfully for what He has revealed to you. Do you now want to become troubled and discouraged again?

ELIZABETH: I acknowledge that the grace God has bestowed upon others is genuine. I am also assured that

God has forgiven me my sins of ignorance (1 Tim. 1:13). But my daily sins, which are not small, but many, great, and grievous, trouble me and almost make me lose heart (Ps. 38:6-8).

DATHENUS: What are you saying, dear Elizabeth? Would you make Christ another Moses again? Is Christ your accuser or your Redeemer, Deliverer, Advocate, and Mediator? Has He only partly forgiven your sins or has He totally and completely forgiven them? Is He a complete or only a half Savior?

Can you not believe that He has forgiven you *all* your sins to the end of your life — yes, until the soul will be parted from the body? Has He canceled and erased the handwriting that was against you? Who then can demand of you any further payment of your debt? Shall God on your behalf yet become unrighteous and demand a double payment? If God accounts you as righteous and Christ intercedes for you, then who can bring any accusation against you?

Has it been all for naught that I have taken so much trouble to instruct and comfort you (Gal. 3:1-4)? Truly, Scripture says very accurately that faith is a gift of God (Eph. 2:8; Phil. 1:29), and that no one will come to Christ unless the person is drawn to Him by the Father (John 6:44).

ELIZABETH: My brother, please be patient with my weakness! I hope that your labor will not prove to be in vain, but as seed must first fall into the earth and die in order to bring forth fruit, so also must the Word you have proclaimed die in my heart before it can take root and bear fruit. Like Mary, the mother of Christ, I will treasure them in my heart and ponder them (Luke 2:19; 11:28).

In the meantime, I believe that I am the greatest sinner in the world.

DATHENUS: I am glad to hear that, and I do not doubt that this Word will bear good fruit in due time. You are right in having such feelings about yourself, for everyone ought to admit with the prodigal son, "Father, I have sinned against heaven and before thee" (Luke 15:18). Therefore Paul was also not ashamed to admit that among all sinners he was the chief of sinners (1 Tim. 1:15).

However, such a confession should not lead to despondency, but rather to the opposite, in order that by way of our shame God's mercy may be magnified. I am sure that your transgression is not the sin that leads to death, of which we spoke earlier.

ELIZABETH: I am sure that the Lord will keep me from that. Despite my weakness, I hope to live and die by the confessed truth of God's Word. Nevertheless, a person is still subject to the law of sin (Rom. 7:25), which is great and grievous.

DATHENUS: That is true, but these are sins not unto death, which believers do not commit, but sin which against their will is in them that accomplishes these things (1 John 5:16, 20). Therefore, as explained above, there is for the children of God no condemnation (Rom. 8:1).

However, in order that you may understand that nothing is happening to you that even the holiest children of God have not experienced and undergone, I shall set before you examples of grievous falls and sins of the most excellent men of God. I do this in order that on the one hand you may learn the greatness of human shortcomings, and on the other hand the great fullness of the mercy that God had shown to them. I hope that as you meditate upon these things, you will experience hope and a lively comfort by faith, together with the workings of the Holy Spirit. For this is the purpose for which the Holy Spirit has caused the very gross sins of God's chosen saints to be recorded.

ELIZABETH: I do want to hear them in order to receive and feel a stronger sense of God's grace toward me.

DATHENUS: I will do this in all simplicity — not to encourage someone to continue in sin (Rom. 6:23), but to demonstrate that we have no reason for boasting (Rom. 3:27; 1 Cor. 1:30). It is for that reason that all glory and praise for our salvation must be ascribed to God (Eph. 2:8-9). I will also show that believers, in similar or more grievous sins, should not despair like Cain (Gen. 4:13). Rather, they should firmly trust that God, for Christ's sake, will surely be gracious to them (Rom. 3:24), and in accordance with His promise will forgive and forget (Ps. 25:7) all their sins, irrespective of how grievous they may be.

ELIZABETH: It should be far from us to despise the children of God when reflecting upon their weaknesses and shortcomings (Mat. 7:4). Who is there who will not find himself involved in the same or similar sins (Ps. 32:5)? Yet for the same reasons that the Holy Spirit has caused these sins to be recorded in writing, we may discuss them. So go ahead; I will listen carefully and whenever I have doubts or questions, I will ask for further explanations.

DATHENUS: You are entitled to this. Yet you should realize beforehand, Elizabeth, that the Holy Spirit did not want to lay before us all the sins and faults of the

saints in the same way that all their virtues are nar-
rated. He has only recorded some transgressions to
show us what all people, no matter how holy, are in
themselves as soon as the Lord withdraws His guid-
ing and restraining hand from them. He also wants to
teach us that they are not saved by the merit of their
own works but by grace alone.

ELIZABETH: I affirm this to be true. If it were all written
down, the world could not contain or comprehend all
the books, as John declares (John 21:25).

DATHENUS: First, it is well-known how upright a man
of God, Noah, was. When all the world had turned
away from God, he found grace in the eyes of the
LORD (Gen. 6:8), and eight people were spared and
preserved in the flood (Gen. 7:8; 1 Pet. 3:20). Peter calls
him a preacher of righteousness (2 Pet. 2:5); Hebrews
refers to him as a reverent man moved by godly fear,
because of his faith (Heb. 11:7).

ELIZABETH: Noah must undoubtedly have been an upright man. Prior to the flood, when he was five hundred
years of age (Gen. 5:12), he discerned and recognized
the condition of the first world. He lived for three
hundred fifty years after the flood (Gen. 9:28). He
witnessed the judgment of God over the entire race.
Thereafter, as another or second Adam, he became the
father of all men upon earth. All the peoples of earth
are descended from him and his children (Gen. 10).

DATHENUS: Despite being the kind of man just described and having seen the fulfillment of what had
been foretold, Noah drank until he was drunk, to
the extent that he lay in his tent naked, thereby
grieving and offending his godly children, while giving wicked Ham occasion to mock him (Gen. 9:21-22).

ELIZABETH: This sin is very common, and many people hardly consider it a sin.

DATHENUS: We must not evaluate sins by the opinions of people, but according to the testimony of God's Word. Paul's words bar from the kingdom of God such transgressors as drunkards, idolaters, adulterers, thieves, and robbers (1 Cor. 6:9-10; Gal. 5:21).

Was not such drunkenness a grievous transgression in Noah, especially considering how he had experienced the wrath of God poured out against the sins of the world (Gen. 7:23), and had been the recipient of the wondrous grace of God? Besides that, the offense he caused his children was no minor sin, as Christ Himself teaches us (Mat. 18:6). Moreover, does not drunkenness lead to many other sins? That is why even some pagan nations have punished the crimes committed during intoxication with a double penalty.

ELIZABETH: I do not want to excuse drunkenness in any way; it causes rational people to behave like irrational beasts. I am therefore as committed an enemy of this sin as I am of all others.

DATHENUS: What drunkenness will do is all too evident from the example of Lot, in spite of the fact that Peter calls him a righteous man who was vexed by the immoral conversation of the wicked (2 Pet. 2:7). His transgressions were indeed very great; especially when we remember that he had seen the terrible manifestation of God's wrath upon Sodom and the other cities (Gen. 19:12). Furthermore, his wife had been turned into a pillar of salt for the sole reason that she had looked back (Gen. 19:26).

Yet Lot made himself so drunk that he fornicated with his own daughters and impregnated them, which was an act of incest of which even the pagans would be ashamed (Lev. 18:6). However, Lot did not only do this once, which was once too often, but the next day he laid with his second daughter and impregnated her also (Gen. 19:32-38). Was not this a grievous sin and a detestable example, such as would drive virtue, honor, and the fear of God from the hearts of his daughters and all others, and drive people away from all godliness?

ELIZABETH: Yes, that did truly happen, but the Scripture says that his daughters did this because they thought there were no more men on earth.

DATHENUS: That excuses neither the daughters nor the father. Human nature should have had an abhorrence of such an act, regardless of whether people ever heard mention made of either God or His commandments.

Yet, I really only want to deal with the crime of Lot whom Peter calls "righteous" (1 Pet. 2:7).

ELIZABETH: Yes, I agree; his transgression was great, detestable, and compounded.

DATHENUS: Nevertheless, Lot is nowhere reproached for this shameful misdeed, nor was it counted against him, which we can see from the inexpressible grace of God upon Lot's children (Deut. 2:9). As soon as they repented toward Him, He made their sins as white as wool (Isa. 1:18.) — yes, even though they were as scarlet as blood which is red and abhorrent.[7]

ELIZABETH: O, the unfathomable depths of God's mercy (Ps. 103:8)! We may rightly say with the prophet, "Who is a God like unto thee, that pardoneth

---

[7] In speaking of the grace of God to Lot's descendants, Dathenus may have had in mind the fact that Lot was an ancestor of the Lord Jesus by his oldest daughter, through Ruth the Moabitess.

iniquity, and passeth by the transgression of the remnant of his heritage? He retaineth not his anger for ever, because he delighteth in mercy. He will turn again, he will have compassion upon us; he will subdue our iniquities; and thou wilt cast all their sins into the depths of the sea" (Micah 7:18-19).

DATHENUS: This God, Elizabeth, has also become your God and Father through Jesus Christ (John 20:17). He is and always remains the same; His Word will always be reliable and true. Therefore, see to it that you give Him fitting honor and learn to maintain a steadfast trust in Him (Isa. 43:10-12).

It would take too long if I were to enumerate the sins and faults of Abraham and all others. Therefore I will only briefly make mention of the noteworthy transgressions of the most prominent children of God (Isa. 54:9).

ELIZABETH: Now watch what you say, Dathenus. Would there be anything in a great saint like Abraham, the father of all the faithful (Rom. 4:16), which rightfully demands punishment? After all, when God called him (Gen. 12:1), didn't he forsake idols (Josh. 24:2)? Did not God make him the glorious promise that in his seed all the families of the earth would be blessed (Gen. 12:3)?

DATHENUS: I know what I am saying, Elizabeth. As Abraham was called and justified by grace (Rom. 3:24), he was likewise also saved by grace (Acts 15:11). Therefore he had nothing in which he could boast before God (Rom. 4:2). Although he was but dust and ashes, yet he found grace with the Lord God (Gen. 12:3).

Are you of the opinion, Elizabeth, that Abraham did not sin? He received God's promises as foretold; however, thereafter he complained impatiently that Eliezer, the son of his handmaid, would be his heir (Gen. 15:3). Later, urged on by the same impatience, he sinned against God's original institution of marriage (Gen. 2:24). He turned from Sarah to Hagar to seek a descendant according to the flesh (Gen. 16:1-4). He also laughed and said in his heart, "Shall a child be born unto him that is an hundred years old? and shall Sarah, that is ninety years old, bear? And Abraham said unto God, O that Ishmael might live before thee!" (Gen. 17:17-18).

Did not Abraham sin? Yes, indeed he did! We also see that even after he was justified, there were still grievous sins and faults in Abraham's life — imperfections such as impatience, unbelief or the doubting of God's promises and omnipotence, following the counsel of the flesh (Gen. 16:2), and laughing at and discrediting God's promises out of unbelief, when God, for the third time, promised him a son out of Sarah (Gen. 17:16-17).

This doubt or unbelief of Abraham is even more evident, for not only did he doubt God's fatherly promises, "You will be blessed and be a blessing"; but being distrustful and ashamed of his wife, he begged her out of unbelief to say that she was his sister (Gen. 12:13).

After he had so manifestly experienced God's fatherly protection, care, and help, he yielded again to the same unbelief and once more put his wife into peril of being defiled, for which he was rightfully rebuked by Abimelech (Gen. 20:1-18).

ELIZABETH: I have never thought about this so carefully or so deeply before. I realize from this example that even among the saints (according to the words of Job) there is no one who is beyond reproach (Job 15:14).

Yet, I believe Abraham's error relative to his marriage to be excusable. After all, Sarah gave Hagar to him as a concubine;[8] thus it was done with Sarah's cooperation and consent.

Concerning Abraham's faith, Paul speaks favorably of him in very clear terms, saying that he did not stagger at the promise of God through unbelief, giving glory to God (Rom. 4:20). Yes, Paul also says that Abraham even believed "in hope against hope"; that is, Abraham hoped when there was no reason to hope (Rom. 4:18), and did not consider his own great age, nor the deadness of Sarah's womb, but he looked to God, being assured that He was able to perform what He had promised (Rom. 4:21).

DATHENUS: I know very well that Sarah gave Hagar to Abraham to be a wife. Elizabeth, the question is, however, whether Sarah, according to God's ordinances, should have done this, and whether Abraham could have followed this carnal advice without committing sin. For example, if you could not have children yourself, could you, without sinning, give your maid to your husband as a second wife, and could he accept her in good conscience?

ELIZABETH: It seems to me that Sarah was permitted to do this, for there was yet no law against it, and where there is no law there is also no transgression.

This has a different meaning to New Testament women, for the Holy Spirit teaches us plainly that every man shall have his own wife and every woman her own husband (1 Cor. 7:2).

---

[8] Dathenus here refers to Hagar as a "huisvrouw" or "wife," but "concubine" is more biblically accurate.

DATHENUS: You truly do not understand this issue correctly. Sarah had no more right or freedom regarding this than the women of the New Testament have. For the ordinance of marriage — the lawful bond of a man and a woman in which two become one flesh, which is Paul's subject — is not just the teaching of Paul (1 Cor. 7), but God has instituted it thus from the beginning. God therefore did not create two or three women for one man but only one woman for one man. Afterwards He declared: "These two shall be one flesh" (Gen. 1:27-28; 2:24). Jesus therefore reminds the Pharisees of the first institution of marriage, saying, "But from the beginning it was not so" (Mat. 19:8).

Even though the law had then not yet been written, Paul states that even from Adam to Moses sin was in the world, whereby death had gained dominion over all people. Where death reigned, there sin must also be, and where sin is, there the law is also present (Rom. 5:13-14). Where there is no law, there is no transgression (Rom. 4:15), as you yourself have admitted.

ELIZABETH: That is a fundamental truth I cannot refute, and so I must admit that Sarah, in giving this counsel out of impatience, and Abraham, in following it, both sinned (Gen. 16:1-4). Nevertheless, Abraham's prayer for Ishmael was heard. God blessed Ishmael (Gen. 17:20) — yes, he saved his life by the wonderful intervention of an angel (Gen. 21:14-20).

DATHENUS: There we see God's great mercy — yes, even to the evil and the ungrateful (Mat. 5:45). If, however, we involve ourselves in that subject matter, we would never exhaust it, for Lot begot two nations by his daughters. Furthermore, Pharez was born as a result of Judah's incestuous act, and Solomon was born to Bathsheba who had been Uriah's wife. Christ, according to His human nature, was brought forth from this lineage.

However, that absolves neither Judah, David, nor Lot. In leaving this subject, however, I must add that later Sarah expelled Hagar and her son, so that Ishmael would not receive the inheritance. However, even though God commanded Abraham to follow Sarah's wishes in this (Gen. 21:10-12), and even though the Holy Spirit testifies that Ishmael was only Abraham's son according to the flesh (Gal. 4:23), you will nevertheless understand that this marriage was not lawful according to the law of God — even though this marriage was lawful according to the social and legal customs of the land and this era.

In fact, Paul calls children who are born in lawful wedlock holy, even when only one of the parties to the marriage is a believer (1 Cor. 7:14).

ELIZABETH: I must admit that I cannot refute that. Yet how do you respond to what I have quoted earlier from Paul concerning Abraham's strong and firm faith?

DATHENUS: What Paul says about Abraham's faith is the truth. Being strengthened by God's grace and power, Abraham believed and his faith was accounted to him for righteousness (Gen. 15:16; Rom. 4:5; Gal. 3:6).

Yet, whenever the Lord had withdrawn His hand from Abraham only a little, he fell into weakness of faith and stumbled. This is confirmed by the following examples: the taking of Hagar, the disgracing and abandoning of his wife, Sarah; and various other matters as mentioned before.

Isaac also fell into doubting God's fatherly care and preservation in spite of what he had observed in his father's life — and also in spite of the promises he himself had received from God (Gen. 26:7-10).

ELIZABETH: O brother, how right Paul is when he says, "What hast thou that thou didst not receive?" (1 Cor. 4:7)! For of ourselves we are not capable of thinking anything good (2 Cor. 3:5). Therefore, as stated before, even the holiest person ought to pray, "Enter not into judgment with thy servant: for in thy sight shall no man living be justified" (Psa. 143:2).

DATHENUS: That is indeed true. For if Job, whom God praises so highly (Job 1:8), admits that he could not answer God once in a thousand times (Job 9:2), then what must we who cannot be compared with Job admit about ourselves? If they are unprofitable servants who have only done that which was commanded them (Luke 17:10), then how unprofitable must we be, who have not kept any commandment perfectly according to God's will!

How can anyone born of woman be pure? Behold, if the moon does not even shine, and the stars are also not pure in His eyes, how much less is a son of man who is but a maggot and a worm? Eliphaz was right when he said, "What is man, that he should be clean? and he which is born of a woman, that he should be righteous? Behold, he putteth no trust in his saints; yea, the heavens are not clean in his sight. How much more abominable and filthy is man, who drinketh iniquity like water?" (Job 15:14-16).

ELIZABETH: That is indeed the matter of which I complained before. Yet Job's friends, who confessed this, were later rebuked by God because they had not spoken what was right. Therefore Job had to sacrifice and pray for them (Job 42:7-9).

DATHENUS: That is true, Elizabeth. They spoke that which was not right in despising and condemning Job as an ungodly person, only because he was so fearfully tried and tested by God. All that time God was not doing this to Job on account of any sins he had committed, but to demonstrate His righteousness to him, and what He may rightly do to people in accordance with His righteousness. He also did this so that He might subsequently show to Job His faithfulness, truth, goodness, and omnipotence, and to hold before all men an example of patience.

However, regarding the evil and corrupted nature of man, and the sin that cleaves to them until death, and which even remains in the holiest of saints against their will, these friends of Job have not professed anything except that which Job also admitted, saying: "Who can bring a clean thing out of an unclean? not one" (Job 14:4). Subsequently, he also confesses, "I uttered that I understood not; things too wonderful for me....Wherefore I abhor myself, and repent in dust and ashes" (Job 42:3, 6).

ELIZABETH: Now I admit, Dathenus, that what you told me in the beginning was true: The greatest perfection a man can attain to in this life consists of a confession of his imperfections.

Please continue your pursuit of this subject, however.

DATHENUS: I will do that. While we are on the subject of Job — was it not a detestable sin for him to have so dreadfully cursed the day of his conception and birth (Job 3:3)? I remind you that he not only did it once on a hasty impulse, but he repeated it a second time, and in spite of the reproof and instruction of his friends, he said, "Wherefore then hast thou brought me forth out of the womb? Oh that I had given up the ghost, and no eye had seen me!" (Job 10:18).

Yet the Lord testifies of Job that there was none like him in the earth, an upright man that feared God and eschewed evil (Job 1:8).

We also see this in the case of Jeremiah who, though God had consecrated from his mother's womb (Jer. 1:4-5), grievously fell into the same sin of blasphemy and impatience. We can read of this very plainly in Jeremiah 20:14-18.

ELIZABETH: Everyone should be aghast at these blasphemous imprecations. Yet these saints, as well as the prophets, fell into these sins. Oh, dear brother, what shall I say about this?

DATHENUS: There is nothing to say about this, dear Elizabeth, except that every mouth must be stopped, and the whole world (Rom. 3:19), that is, all people, must be included under sin and disobedience, so that He might have mercy on all (Rom. 11:32).

ELIZABETH: Yes, that is indeed true, and all these examples demonstrate it more than sufficiently. However, please state the rest of this teaching by way of a short summary.

DATHENUS: I will do that as well as I can. Jacob was a very godly man, but did not an infirm faith often cause him to doubt? Yet that was only the least of his faults, since he was also guilty of serious misconduct in marriage. He not only had two sisters at the same time for his wives (Gen. 29:16-30), but he also entered into wedlock with two maids (Gen. 30:3-4, 9). That was not only contrary to the law of the Lord (Lev. 18:16), but also contrary to human nature.

From being married to four women at the same

time, we may deduce the corruptions of Jacob's nature that remained in him, notwithstanding the fact that he was a child of God and a holy patriarch (Exo. 3:6) who, as Christ testifies, sits with Abraham and Isaac in the kingdom of God (Mat. 8:11; 22:32; Luke 13:28). Yes, God consistently calls Himself the God of Abraham, Isaac, and Jacob.

ELIZABETH: Yes, this is indeed a great wonder in the holy Jacob! Yet we do not read that he was reproved for those things or that they were ever accounted as sins against him. Therefore I believe that this polygamy was permitted at the time of the patriarchs for two reasons. First, because by these means God was pleased to multiply the seed of Abraham as the sand of the sea, in accordance with His promises (Gen. 15:5; 22:17). Secondly, because the believers of the Old Testament were still a coarse, carnal people who had not attained to the same degree of perfection as the people of the New Testament dispensation. Therefore Christ may justly demand a greater measure of perfection from those in the New Testament.

DATHENUS: Dear Elizabeth, how long will you remain mired in this misunderstanding? Have I not rendered sufficient proof to you earlier that everything that conflicts with the original institution of marriage (Gen. 1:27, 2:24) is sin? Must a person sin against God's ordinances and debase marriage in order that God's promises be really and truly fulfilled? Are we to do evil that good may come (Rom. 3:8)?

Have you also forgotten, what I explained to you earlier at length, that Christ is neither another Moses nor a new lawgiver (John 5:45), but that He, delivering us from the power and curse of the law, only uses the law as a schoolmaster and guide to bring us to Himself (Gal. 3:15, 24)?

Are you of the opinion that the children of Abraham can be holier and more perfect than their father? Are not the saints of the Old Testament held before us as models and examples for us to follow? Elizabeth! How long will you remain mired in this misapprehension, in spite of all my instruction?

ELIZABETH: Yes, I must confess and deplore my poor memory and foolishness. For if I consider the matter rightly, Christ can require nothing more perfect than the expression of the new man or the image of God (Col. 3:10) in which man was created in the beginning (Gen. 1:27). Therefore, whatever does not harmonize with the prescribed likeness of God impressed upon man in his creation (Eph. 4:24) must be sin and unrighteousness, no matter who the person may be in whom these sins are found. Thus, I will no longer justify or exonerate anyone, but in seeing their sins and faults, I will confess and mourn the imperfection of all people (Gal. 5:17). Furthermore, I will also confess and mourn my own imperfections and extol the great grace of God who has neither rejected nor condemned them and me for these sins, but has adopted us as His children (John 1:12; Rom. 8:16-17) and saved us (Ps. 103:12).

But please go on. From here on I will not hinder you much.

DATHENUS: Now you understand this correctly, Elizabeth, and thus I will continue unhindered. Regarding the incest of Judah, I have said enough about it earlier. Being in authority, he wanted to punish another with death for the sin he himself had committed (Gen. 38:24).

What shall I say of Aaron, the Levitical priest, who besides other sins, made a golden calf and not only permitted the detestable idolatry, but also erected it himself (Exo. 32:1-6)?

What about Moses, that upright and eminent servant of God (Num. 12:7), who finally fell into unbelief (1 Cor. 10:12) and was not permitted to enter the promised land (Num. 20:12; Deut. 34:4-5)? Such sins may be considered small sins by some, but that does not keep them from being grievous and detestable before God. They are violations of the first table of the law (Exo. 20:3-5).

ELIZABETH: Certainly, we must admit that there are no greater sins committed than unbelief and idolatry (1 Cor. 6:9; 10:7). Yet, I also believe that even though both Aaron and Moses were punished by physical death and exclusion from the land of Canaan, they still received forgiveness of sins, true righteousness, and eternal salvation by faith in Jesus Christ (Mat. 17:3; John 3:16).

DATHENUS: That is entirely beyond doubt. However, these examples serve to affirm that there can be no sin — either against the first or the second table — for which God does not have a far greater grace to forgive His children (Isa. 1:18), when they confess and deplore their sins (Ps. 51) and in true faith ask forgiveness in Christ's Name (Luke 15:10-24; 1 John 1:9).

ELIZABETH: That is also entirely my sentiment, and the only sure comfort for troubled consciences (Ps. 32:1-2; Rom. 4:7).

DATHENUS: That is so. But to continue, Samson was also set apart and consecrated to the Lord (Judg. 13:5). In the New Testament he is counted among those who serve as an example for us to follow (Heb. 11:32). Yet his history contains astonishing elements. First, against the counsel of his parents, he took a woman of Timnath, (Judg. 14:1-7) the daughter of an uncircumcised Philistine, to wife. Thereafter, by tying foxes together by their tails with burning brands, he destroyed the crops of the Philistines, giving them due cause to burn his wife and her father (Judg. 15:1-6). Next, he went to Gaza and consorted with a harlot, and finally ended his life as well as that of the Philistines (Judg. 16).

Are those not remarkably gruesome incidents? Yet, in spite of these things, he was a man of God, whose actions God used to the good — yes, His Name was glorified and exalted by them.

ELIZABETH: How marvelous and merciful is our God! He can bring light out of darkness (Gen. 1:3; 1 Cor. 4:6) and good out of evil.

DATHENUS: Yes, that is so. The example of David, of whom God testifies that he was a man after His own heart (1 Sam. 13:14), shows this even more clearly. Yet David himself confesses and deplores his sins to be very great (Ps. 25:11), stating also that as a heavy burden they weighed him down (Ps. 38:1-8) — yes, that they were more numerous than the hairs of his head (Ps. 40:12). He does not say much here about his inward sins, which people could have neither observed nor punished, but were known only to God and himself. Therefore, it is not necessary to describe the multiplicity and magnitude of his sins with many words.

Yet this alone is noteworthy: David was called to be a prophet and a king. Being qualified for and anointed to these offices by the Holy Spirit (1 Sam. 16:13), he received the promises of Christ who was to be born from his seed (Ps. 2:7, 12), and he prophesied and wrote so gloriously of Christ. Nevertheless, David also committed so many gross and palpable sins: He became so angry at Nabal's insensitivity and stupidity that he intended to massacre all males in Nabal's house (1 Sam. 25:10). In God's eyes this would have been a very cruel and murderous deed to have killed so many innocent people.

ELIZABETH: Yet David confessed that sin, and thanks be to God, he was stopped from carrying out his intention (1 Sam. 25:23-26).

DATHENUS: It is not pertinent to the pursuit of our subject whether David confessed his sin. We are only demonstrating that David committed great sins after having received the Holy Spirit.

We also see that even though David clearly experienced God's help and preservation (1 Sam. 21-22), he became so cowardly when he became imperiled that he ran to God's enemies and presented himself as an insane person (1 Sam. 21:10-15). He crossed over to Israel's enemies not only once, but twice (1 Sam. 27:1-2), without asking counsel from God's mouth — all this to the sorrow and offense of God's people and the joy of the enemies. Was not this also a great transgression?

However, David's debasement and desecration of marriage can also in no wise be excused. He had married Michal, the daughter of Saul, but later married Abigail, the widow of Nabal. Then, still not being satisfied, he married Ahinoam of Jezreel (1 Sam. 25:40-44). Besides that, he also married, against God's law (Deut. 7:3), Maacha, the daughter of the king of Geshur who became the mother of Absalom. This was a marriage relationship which God had expressly forbidden. Still not satisfied, he married Haggith, Abital, and Eglah (2 Sam. 3:2-5). Besides that, we know that David also had ten concubines (2 Sam. 15:16) [also see Deut. 17:17]. In spite of all that, David committed adultery with Bathsheba, the wife of Uriah, his faithful servant.

However, not only did David commit adultery, but he slyly arranged that good man's death — yes, doing so deliberately and treacherously, causing the death of many of God's people. After this crime, he showed no repentance, living on and laboring as if he had done no wrong — until Nathan reproved and rebuked him for it.

Is not this a compilation of many and grievous sins? Yet, when he confessed his sins, he was comforted by the prophet with the words, "The LORD also hath put away thy sin; thou shalt not die" (2 Sam. 12:13).

ELIZABETH: The Lord has hereby certainly demonstrated the truth of His Word when He says: "For I have no pleasure in the death of him that dieth, saith the Lord GOD: wherefore turn yourselves, and live ye" (Ezek. 18:32). Yet it does not seem that David transgressed in many other sins, the exception being his degradation of marriage.

DATHENUS: Even though this were so, was this sin not enough reason for God to banish him from before His face and to damn him forever?

ELIZABETH: This would indeed have been the case if God had dealt with David according to His justice! David therefore pleaded so humbly for grace rather than for justice (Ps. 6:1, 38:1, 61:1, 143:2).

DATHENUS: Yet David also committed many other sins, as we have mentioned earlier. Was it not a striking injustice and an act of tyranny toward Mephibosheth, the son of Jonathan (2 Sam. 4:4) — the Jonathan who had loved him so faithfully (1 Sam. 18:1) and remained faithful to him at the peril of his own life and limbs (1 Sam. 18) — that after having given Mephibosheth all his father's goods and lands, he confiscated his property without even giving Mephibosheth a hearing, doing so merely on the basis of the false accusation of the servant of Mephibosheth (2 Sam. 16:1-4)?

ELIZABETH: Indeed, there David sinned against the law of God in two ways: First, contrary to the law of God, he passed sentence on the testimony of only one witness; secondly, he did not first summon the accused before him to make a defense (Deut. 19:15-18). That is the duty of judges, for else who in this world could be exonerated or whose life would be safe?

DATHENUS: Even the Gentile nations have understood that God has given a person two ears so that not only one party but both parties would be heard and a righteous judgment be rendered.

Yet it is not my purpose to recite all the sins of David which he himself has not been able to count nor discern (Ps. 19:12; 40:12); his many other faults have therefore been omitted.

Was that not a grievous sin that he allowed himself to be moved by Satan (1 Chr. 21:1), so that while trusting in his own might, he caused the people to be numbered, even when his own courtiers so faithfully and firmly advised against it (2 Sam. 24:1-4)? The severity of the punishment that this brought upon the people shows us the magnitude of this offense: Seventy thousand people died in Israel of the pestilence (1 Chr. 21:24). Before God, David was primarily guilty of these deaths.

ELIZABETH: This was certainly a grievous sin, as the severity of the penalty confirms. Yet the people must also have sinned against God, and thus it was not solely David's fault.

DATHENUS: The guilt of the people does not exonerate David. The rebuke by the prophet Gad and the choice of three punishments, show clearly enough that he was the cause of the very gruesome punishment the people had to bear. That is why David absolves the poor people as being only sheep, and he takes the blame entirely upon himself, acknowledging that he had acted very foolishly (1 Chr. 21:10-17; 2 Sam. 24).

ELIZABETH: The fact that David, being such a horrible sinner, was yet saved, does indeed clearly reflect the inexpressible mercy and grace of God. This shows us very clearly that God, as a Father, is merciful to His penitent children.

DATHENUS: Not only was David saved in the end, Elizabeth, but notwithstanding his being laden with many sins and misdeeds, he was still one of the foremost kings, prophets, and servants of God. There were very few of the kings who followed after him who even came to the degree of excellence as David had (1 Ki. 15:3; 2 Ki. 14:3; 2 Chr. 28:1). Therefore, we read that those kings who walked in his footsteps are praised (2 Chr. 34:1-2).

Elizabeth, in concluding our consideration of David, please observe that in spite of the great number of his sins (as we have already shown to be the case) the Holy Spirit nevertheless testifies that David did that which was pleasing to God all his days, except in the matter of Uriah the Hittite (1 Sam. 15:5). Here David is accused of only one crime, even though he himself testifies very differently, as we have shown earlier. Elsewhere God fully exonerates David when He, in rebuking Jereboam by the prophet Ahijah, says, "...thou hast not been as my servant David, who kept my commandments, and who followed me with all his heart, to do that only which was right in mine eyes" (1 Ki. 14:8).

Is it not a wonder above wonders that God finds nothing worthy of punishment or condemnation in David and praises him so highly, whereas David so often accuses and condemns himself (Ps. 51:4)?

ELIZABETH: Oh Dathenus, the unsearchable goodness of God is beyond the understanding of all people — yes, even of all the angels!

Now I understand why David defines man's salvation as consisting in the forgiveness, covering, and nonimputation of sins (Ps. 32:1-2). Truly, Paul drew the right conclusion when he said, "If God is for us, who can be against us?" (Rom. 8:31). "It is God that justifieth. Who is he that condemneth?" (Rom. 8:33-34).

But tell me, Dathenus, seeing that David was such a wretched sinner, why does God still call him a man after His own heart (1 Sam. 13:14)? Why are they praised who followed in his footsteps? Why does the Lord absolve him and also praise him? What unusual virtues did the Lord find in him by which David so greatly pleased Him?

DATHENUS: David had absolutely no inherent virtues, for he was born in sin and conceived in iniquity (Ps. 51:5). However, the Lord, by His Holy Spirit, graciously granted and implanted many glorious virtues in David: a saving knowledge through the Messiah Christ Jesus; a pure love to God; a strong, firm, and immovable faith; trust in God with a burning love; a zeal for God's Word; a pure religion; patience and submission in crossbearing; unfeigned love for his neighbor; being humble and lowly in his own eyes — even in the days of his exaltation and majesty — and more virtues like them.

Yet all these, and whatever virtues David had, were all given him by God out of grace. God loved David for Christ Jesus' sake, just as He loves all His chosen — yes, He has loved them all for His own Name's sake (Eph. 1:5).

Moses also testifies that God loved Israel and their seed for that very reason, and chose them for His own (Deu. 4:37; 10:15). What moved God to love Jacob and choose him while he was still in his mother's body, before he had done good or evil (Rom. 9:10-13)? Likewise, Paul tells us that God has saved us, as well as called us with a holy calling — not according to our works but according to His own purpose and grace, which was given us in Christ Jesus before the ages began (2 Tim. 1:9).

ELIZABETH: Oh, the inexpressible goodness of God! He does not love us because of anything that is in us, but for His own Name's sake! I thus perceive that God begins, performs, and completes everything in His children only for His Name's sake, so that His goodness and mercy might be revealed, known, and praised through us.

DATHENUS: You have grasped this well. Paul therefore calls the children of God "vessels of mercy," in which God has willed to make known the glorious treasure of His grace and the riches of His glory (Rom. 9:23).

But we would run short of time if we tried to examine and explain the other lessons in the histories of Solomon, Asa, Jehoshaphat, Ezekiel, Manasseh, Josiah, Jeremiah, Jonah, and many other children of God. All these, because they were God's children out of grace, for Christ's sake, were saved by faith alone and not of works (Acts 15:11; Heb. 11:3, 9; Eph. 2:8-9) — yes, even though they were laden with many grievous sins. The prophetic writings clearly bear witness to this (Isa. 64:6; Dan. 9:8).

ELIZABETH: That is beyond contradiction. That is why John the Baptist so rightly says, "...of His fullness have all we received and grace for grace" (John 1:16).

But tell me, Dathenus, how is it that you also place and count Solomon among the elect children of God, when almost all scholars consider him to be among the lost?

DATHENUS: Do you wonder about this, Elizabeth? But why do those scholars count Solomon among the lost? What reasons do they have for this?

ELIZABETH: O brother, you would almost cause me to be troubled. What a question that is to ask me! Would you count such a man among the children of God, who, against God's will and God's expressed command, had such a great number of wives and concubines (Deut. 17:17; 1 Ki. 11:3)? For he had seven hundred wives as queens, and three hundred concubines besides. Also, in his old age these women moved and seduced his heart to idols, for which he constructed high places or temples.

Therefore the Lord was angry with him, and tore the kingdom from the hand of his son. Since we do not read of Solomon's repentance, what hope can you have of his salvation?

DATHENUS: All that you have told of Solomon's grievous sins is very true, Elizabeth. Solomon sinned very
grievously in taking so many wives and concubines
(Deu. 17:17). Yet, as we have shown earlier, Jacob
(Gen. 29:30) and David (2 Sam. 15:16) were also guilty
of these sins. Yet the sin of Lot was even more abominable, as we have shown earlier, and yet he is called
"the righteous Lot" (2 Pet. 2:7).

It was indeed a detestable sin when Solomon allowed his wives to seduce him into idolatry (1 Ki.
11:4-9). Have we not observed earlier, however, how
Aaron fell into the same sin (Exo. 32:24), and that he
was yet numbered among God's children?

Regarding idolatry, did not Manasseh far exceed
Solomon in this sin? For he not only erected idol
altars, but also introduced all kinds of fortune-telling
and witchcraft (2 Ki. 21:2-9). He also sacrificed his
children by fire to idols — yes, he led Jerusalem and
all Judea so far into sin that they became worse than
the pagans themselves. Nevertheless, he received
grace and forgiveness of sins (2 Chr. 33:2-13), even
though he shed much innocent blood (2 Ki. 21:16) —
something Solomon never did.

ELIZABETH: Oh, how unsearchable is the mercy which
God bestowed upon Manasseh! Paul was therefore
correct when he stated that where sin abounded,
grace did much more abound (Rom. 5:20).

In Manasseh's case we ought not be so surprised,
however, for Scripture tells of his contrition and repentance (2 Chr. 33:12-13). What reason do you have,
however, for having such secure hopes of Solomon's
salvation?

DATHENUS: I have very weighty and sound reasons.

First of all, there are God's promises and His great grace. Are you of the opinion, Elizabeth, that Solomon died in impenitence and therefore was damned, just because it is not written anywhere that he repented? Where do you read anything of the penitence of Lot, Jacob, or Samson — or of Josiah who brought God's people into great peril, and who willfully and against all warnings cast himself into the jaws of death (2 Chr. 35:21-23)?

I will explain the reasons, however, that move me to firmly hope and surely to believe in Solomon's salvation. First of all, the book named Ecclesiastes is certainly written by Solomon. For many reasons this is an irrefutable fact. He was king over Israel at Jerusalem (Eccl. 1:12), and had houses, gardens and parks, riches, treasures and glory — more than all who ruled prior to him in Jerusalem (Eccl. 2:4-9). Yet he confesses that all that is in the world is vanity, and after many moving exhortations to patience, dying to the world, and holiness of life, gives a beautiful testimony to the origin and immortality of souls, and closes his book with these words: "Fear God, and keep his commandments: for this is the whole duty of man" (Eccl. 12:13), stating that is the essence of all doctrine. Reading this, who can doubt that he had repented of his vain and sinful life when he wrote that book?

ELIZABETH: O brother, now you have comforted and reassured my heart; for I never before heard it told like this nor so thoroughly thought out. But please continue.

DATHENUS: Another reason is the promises given to David concerning his son, namely, that he would sit after him on his throne. Even though we should understand and explain them as speaking primarily of Christ, the true Solomon (Mat. 12:24), the words, "if he commits iniquity, I will chasten him with the rods of men, and with the blows of the sons of men," cannot be applied to the sinless Christ, but must be understood as applying necessarily to Solomon, as also what follows, "But my mercy shall not depart from him, as I took it from Saul, whom I put away before thee" (2 Sam. 7:12-16).

The Holy Spirit sufficiently proved that this is so, for He testifies that God spoke to Solomon, saying: "Forasmuch as this is done of thee, and thou hast not kept my covenant and my statutes, which I have commanded thee, I will surely rend the kingdom from thee, and will give it to thy servant. Notwithstanding in thy days I will not do it for David thy father's sake: but I will rend it out of the hand of thy son" (1 Ki. 11:11-12).

These are the rods of men and the blows of the sons of men with which God threatened David's son. God nevertheless promises that He will not take His mercy from him, as David also says elsewhere (Ps. 89:30-36).

ELIZABETH: Those reasons are truly weighty and sound. Why would some people want to deny and refuse Solomon God's grace, seeing how God had promised it to him in such fatherly terms? The reasons you mentioned earlier, as well as the fact that he wrote the book of Ecclesiastes after his repentance (as has sufficiently been proven before), which contains an open confession of his guilt and exhortations to seek salvation, moves me to firmly trust that Solomon died a blessed death and has also been saved.

However, tell me brother, what is the main purpose and usefulness of this example of Solomon?

DATHENUS: First of all, Elizabeth, we have his example in order that we might humble ourselves under the

mighty hand of God (1 Pet. 5:6) and learn to acknowledge our weakness and insignificance more and more.
As soon as God withdraws His hand from us, no
matter how wonderfully and richly God has endowed
us with gifts, we fall very grievously (2 Cor. 3:5; John
15:4) — as the examples of David (2 Sam. 11:4: 24:1-2)
and Solomon teach us. David indeed spoke in truth
when he said, "Surely men of low degree are vanity."
Men of high degree are equally fallible; they also
weigh less than nothing (Ps. 62:9).

However, these instances teach us at once that however great the sins of God's children may be, God's
grace abounds even more to forgive them (Ps. 103:3)
when they ask Him for forgiveness through Jesus
Christ (Ezek. 18:32; Ps. 51:4; Rom. 5:20). The conduct
of the father of the prodigal son indeed confirms this
to us, for the father saw his son while he was still afar
off; and moved by compassion, he ran to his son, fell
on his neck, and kissed him (Luke 15:20; Isa. 65:24).

ELIZABETH: Oh yes, such glorious lessons are to be
learned from the account of Solomon's fall and repentance! Dear brother, by God's grace and Word you have
dressed the wounds of my troubled and imprisoned
heart and set me free. You have poured the oil of
gladness abundantly upon my dejected heart and refreshed it. If this good God is for us, "who can be
against us?" (Rom. 8:31).

There is still one question I want to ask you. Will
God in the New Testament dispensation still show
such grace to His children, seeing He has given them
a greater knowledge of His will and commandments?
Are there any instances of this?

DATHENUS: What are you asking me now, Elizabeth?

Would the coming of Christ have diminished God's grace? Would God turn His fatherly heart away from us after having adopted us in Jesus Christ and in grace and mercy as His children (John 1:12; Gal. 4:6; John 1:16-17) — yes, as joint heirs with Christ (Rom. 8:17)? Who would, or can, doubt God's love toward us, when the Father loves us with the same love with which He loves Christ, His only begotten Son (John 17:23; Heb. 1:14)?

ELIZABETH: Oh, why am I still so filled with doubts, and troubled and sickly? However, I pray with the father of the demoniac, "Lord, I believe, help thou mine unbelief" (Mark 9:24); and with Christ's apostles: "Lord, increase our faith" (Luke 17:5).

DATHENUS: That is a good prayer. Such prayers ascend to God and penetrate the clouds (Ps. 141:2). Christ invites and desires those who have such broken and contrite hearts (Ps. 51:17; Isa. 66:2; Mat. 5:6; Mat. 11:28; 12:20), but not those who consider themselves holy and perfect.

However, in order to bring this treatise to a conclusion, you do understand, dear Elizabeth, as I explained earlier, that it never really was the intent of the Holy Spirit in the writing of Holy Scripture to give us a description of the sins and faults of God's children (Rom. 7:17). Instead, it is God's purpose to bring us to the knowledge of God and Jesus Christ (Mark 5:6; Luke 24:27) and to exhort us most diligently to a godly Christian life.

Still, to promote your peace of heart, I will do briefly what you have asked of me for your increased reassurance (Ps. 14:7; John 5:39). Do you not perceive and observe how Zacharias, the father of John the Baptist, whom God terms "righteous" and "blameless," fell into unbelief — which is the greatest of all sins — right after that? Because of that, God struck him dumb for nine months (Luke 1:6, 20).

Have you not seen how the believers in the church of Corinth, whom Paul calls "sanctified in Christ and called to be saints" (1 Cor. 1:2), not only were defiled with quarrels and factions (1 Cor. 1:10-11), but also with shameful and offensive intermingling with idolaters (1 Cor. 6:1-2)? Yes, they even corrupted themselves with a shameful abuse of the Lord's Supper (1 Cor. 11:18-22). However, they tolerated such sexual immorality as was not even named among the pagans, that a man has his father's wife (1 Cor. 5:1; 7:2). It is true indeed that Paul commanded such a man to be cut off. Yet, since he repented, he was not excommunicated. Paul commanded the very opposite — that he should be accepted again and comforted (2 Cor. 2:6-7).

The sins of the churches of Asia, which the Holy Spirit described and rebuked, were also very great — as, for example, the church of Ephesus who lost her first love (Rev. 2:4). The church of Pergamos included some who disseminated the shameful doctrine of the Nicolaitans (Rev. 2:14-15). Thyatira accepted false prophets and prophetesses, whom Christ compares to Jezebel (Rev. 2:20) — a most detestable sin. Those of Laodicea were neither cold nor hot, but they gloried as being rich and having no want. Nevertheless, they were miserable, blind, and naked (Rev. 3:16-17).

Still, in spite of these very evident sins and faults, the Lord does not reject them but He urges them to repentance and improvement; meanwhile, He retains and acknowledges them as His churches and very beloved children. He calls them to perseverance by holding before them various precious promises and admonitions (Rev. 2:5-7, 16-17, 23-28; 3:18-21).

If you diligently read the epistles of the apostles, you will often come across similar sins in the believing children of God. That is why they are also exhorted to put off the old man, to put their earthly members to death, such as fornication, evil desires, greed, and other such sins (Eph. 4:22; Col. 3:5). These admonitions would serve no purpose if it were not for the presence of such sins. Yet, in spite of this, the Holy Spirit addresses them as holy, believing, and beloved children of God (Eph. 1:5; Col. 1:2).

ELIZABETH: What shall I reply to this? Whichever way we turn and move, we also find such sins and faults in the holiest of people (Job 4:18, 14:4). David certainly spoke truthfully when he said, "They are all gone aside, they are all together become filthy: there is none that doeth good, no, not one" (Ps. 14:2-3; 53:2-3).

DATHENUS: That is what we just talked about; for if the servant who did all that his Lord required of him must admit that he is only an unprofitable servant, what must we think of ourselves, who do not fulfill even one commandment of our Lord uprightly?

To get back to our subject, however, let us look at Peter, and in his person, at all the apostles: Do you remember how that after Christ called him (Mat. 4:18-19) and after he prepared Christ's way by preaching (Mat. 10:5-7) — yes, after he had so gloriously confessed Christ, for which Christ called him blessed, that he immediately afterward went astray, so that Christ called him "Satan" (Mat. 16:16, 23), Peter being full of worldly and fleshly opinions? Do you also remember how he forsook and denied Christ, and when Christ was resurrected, he with the other disciples were so slow to believe it? After he had received the Holy Spirit, was he not guilty of shameful hypocrisy and pretense (Gal. 2:11-14)? What does Peter have to boast about?

ELIZABETH: Nothing at all. Peter is indeed correct when, rejecting the unbearable yoke of the law of Moses, he says, "But we believe that through the grace of the Lord Jesus Christ we shall be saved, even as they" (Acts 15:11).

DATHENUS: You understand this correctly. John the Baptist was filled with the Holy Spirit in his mother's womb (Luke 1:41) and was the greatest among those born of women (Mat. 11:11). He includes himself in the number of those who are saved solely by grace, and says: "And of His fullness have all we received, and grace for grace" (John 1:16). He also includes himself in the words, "The Lamb of God which taketh away the sin of the world" (John 1:29).

Mary, the mother of Christ, being of the same mind, also delights in God her Savior, and in faith looked upon the blessed Seed that God had promised Abraham. Therefore she also is called "blessed" (Luke 1:45-48) because of her faith (Luke 11:28).

Although the sins of all the saints are not shown us, for the reasons given earlier, yet all humans are by nature children of wrath and of death (Eph. 2:3, 5), and the whole world is guilty before God (Rom. 3:19). Therefore, all those who are saved receive this salvation by grace (Eph. 2:8). Christ thus speaks of all who are His sheep who enter by Him who is the door, "I give unto them eternal life: and they shall never perish, neither shall any man pluck them out of my hand" (John 10:28).

ELIZABETH: That point has been proven so abundantly and exhaustively that it would be a disgrace to desire further proof. Dathenus, I thank you from my heart for the trouble you have taken and for your great diligence. Yet, I hope that it will not offend you if I ask you to repeat this instruction in a short summary, just to strengthen my weak memory and to give me comfort.

DATHENUS: That will not offend me at all, and I will sum up the whole matter in two points:

First, you should know and understand that all expressions and utterances in Holy Scripture which require something of us that is outside the boundaries of our ability or our free will, whether we find them in the Old or in the New Testament (regardless of whether they are pressed upon us by Moses, Christ, or Paul), contain the law and serve as a guide or director to lead us to Christ (2 Cor. 3:5; Phil. 2:13; John 15:4; Gal. 3:2). The perfect compliance that such Scriptures require of us, we must not seek and find in ourselves but in Christ; otherwise we will never have any enduring comfort or assurance (Phil. 3:9; 2 Cor. 12:9).

However, we must be satisfied with the measure of divine grace He has given us, even though in the flesh we still serve sin against our will; that is, that part of us that is not yet the new born-again nature (Rom. 7:16-17). We may be assured that in spite of this there is nothing to condemn in us because we are in Christ (Rom. 8:1), who is the end of the law (Rom. 10:4) and has delivered us from its power and curse (Gal. 3:13). Yes, He destroyed it by hanging on and being nailed to His cross (Col. 2:14). Thus, by the law we are dead to the law and have nothing to do with the law, but are now married to another husband, namely Jesus

Christ (Rom. 7:4). We must voluntarily serve Him in love, according to the gifts and grace which God gives us through the Holy Spirit; not in the old life of the letter that kills and condemns, but in a new life (Rom. 7:6; 2 Cor. 3:6) by the spirit of adoption as God's children (Rom. 8:15).

ELIZABETH: There you have indeed given me a brief and comprehensive summary of the first point about the law and the gospel. Yes, it is true, if we honestly examine ourselves in light of the law of God, we find nothing in us except death and condemnation. Therefore, we must seek the peace and serenity of our consciences outside of ourselves only in Jesus Christ, for He is our peace (Eph. 2:14).

DATHENUS: Yes, that has been shown clearly and sufficiently from Paul's words. Therefore he also says elsewhere that God, through Christ, has given us all things (Rom. 8:32; 5:1). How can a person lack anything who has all things in Christ?

The second point concerns eternal salvation. This is not awarded us either wholly or in part for our works, but only from God's grace by faith in Christ Jesus (Eph. 2:8-9; 2 Tim. 1:9; John 1:12).

Learn to understand this from the example of the two thieves who were crucified with Jesus. They were both condemned to death for the same crimes. But even though they were equal in regard to their sins and their deserved punishment upon sin, God does not treat them equally, but yet very justly. God allows the one to remain hardened due to his righteous judgment and to die in that condition; the other one He inclines by His grace to be sincerely sorrowful for his sins, resulting in a knowledge of and a sincere petition to Jesus Christ, to be followed by eternal salvation (Eph. 2:5). God still deals in this manner with the children of men, who in and of themselves are sinners equally deserving of death. Some He judges according to His hidden righteous judgments, permitting them to remain and die in sin and unbelief (Rom. 9:17-18), whereas others He receives in grace and saves them (Luke 23:39-43).

This Christ also teaches us when He says that He is not praying for the world (John 17:9) but rather sacrifices Himself for those who are given Him out of the world, so that they may be sanctified to eternity (John 17:19), even though they are and will always remain poor sinners as long as they are in this life.

In summary, just as there was no real difference between the two thieves, so there is no difference between the children of Adam as to their corrupted natures. According to God's righteous judgment, one remains hardened and obstinate, and the other, out of pure grace, is brought to the knowledge of sin and faith in Jesus Christ. So it goes with the entire human race (Rom. 5:12-18).

ELIZABETH: I fully concur with this. I consider the case of the two thieves to be identical to the case of Jacob and Esau (Gen. 25:22; Rom. 9:12-13) which you discussed earlier. This also teaches us that God dispenses His benefits freely and without compulsion, for He graciously gives the same wage to him who has labored for only one hour as He does to those who have labored all day in the heat of the day (Mat. 20:1-16).

DATHENUS: Your understanding is correct, for had the penitent thief ever done anything good in his entire life? Indeed not! Yet Christ says to him, "To day shalt thou be with me in paradise" (Luke 23:43). For a person is justified by faith, without the deeds of the law (Rom. 3:28). Therefore he who boasted of his daily labors was cast out (Mat. 20:11-14).

Paul expresses this very pointedly: "Israel hath not obtained that which he seeketh for; but the election hath obtained it, and the rest were blinded" (Rom. 11:7). God will graciously forgive all the trespasses of those who heartily humble themselves — whether it be a matter of ten thousand talents, five hundred pennies, or only fifty cents (Mat. 18:24-28). Therefore both John the Baptist and the penitent thief must acknowledge, magnify, and praise God's grace and mercy, which can be fully understood from the foregoing.

Is there anything else about this matter, dear sister, that still oppresses and troubles your conscience?

ELIZABETH: No, praise God. You have fully met my needs with God's Word, and thus all reason for discouragement has been removed (Acts 11:14). I pray God that I may keep His Word, having opened my heart to understand it so well that even Satan cannot snatch it away from my heart (Mat. 13:19; Luke 10:42). I pray that it may bring forth abundant fruit in me (Mat. 13:23), so that I may demonstrate my childlike gratitude to God with a joyful spirit and in godly love use my Christian liberty well (Rom. 8:15; Gal. 5:13) to the edification of my neighbor (Ps. 51:13-14).

DATHENUS: Not only will the eternal God, the Giver of every good gift (James 1:17), as James calls Him, grant this to us, but He will do so to all His chosen children (John 1:12). Nevertheless, we must always confess that we are and remain debtors as long as we are in this life (Rom. 13:8). We must also use these means

Christ instructs us to use to be delivered and acquitted of our guilt (Mat. 6:12, 18:26; Luke 11:4); that is, by faith we are to appropriate Christ, who has taken all our sins upon Himself (Isa. 53:6), paid them in full, and nailed the handwriting that was against us to His cross (Col. 2:14). Thus, in Christ, we are justified of grace (Rom. 3:24) and have the righteousness that is valid and accredited before God (Phil. 3:9).

ELIZABETH: I hope both to live and to die by this — yes, to adhere to it steadfastly.

DATHENUS: Christ desires this of us when he compares Himself with the brazen serpent that was lifted up in the wilderness (Num. 21:8-9). He teaches us that the Israelites, upon being mortally bitten, were not healed or restored to health by medicines or bandages but only by looking at the brazen serpent upon God's command; likewise he teaches us that we also can never be delivered or saved except by spiritually looking to the crucified Christ alone (John 3:14-15); that is, by a steadfast and heartfelt trust in Him (John 3:15-16; Gal. 2:20).

He alone is the way, the truth, and the life, and no one comes to the Father except by Him alone (John 14:6), because upon earth no other name has been given among men by which we can be saved (Acts 4:12). Therefore Paul is correct when he states that there is one God and one Mediator between God and man, namely, Jesus Christ (1 Tim. 2:5).

ELIZABETH: My beloved Christ alone is my all in all. He truly is my wisdom and righteousness, sanctification and redemption (1 Cor. 1:30; John 17:17-19). Therefore, when David speaks of his God whom he beheld and knew in Christ the Messiah, he says, "My flesh and my heart faileth: but God is the strength of my heart and my portion for ever" (Ps. 73:26). This I also say when I languish or pine or am ready to perish. Christ is my only comfort, solace, and great gain (Phil. 1:21; 1 Tim. 6:6).

DATHENUS: The Lord will keep you steadfast and immovable (1 Cor. 15:58; 2 Tim. 4:5a; Zech. 10:12) in this faith and firm trust, and uphold you until the very end, so that you may finally say, "I have fought a good fight, I have finished my course, I have kept the faith. Henceforth there is laid up for me a crown of righteousness" (2 Tim. 4:7-8).

ELIZABETH: Amen! Amen! I know whom I have believed and am convinced that He is able to keep my portion or inheritance (Acts 20:32) until that day (2 Tim. 1:12), trusting that He who has begun the good work in me will perfect it until the day of Jesus Christ (Phil. 1:6).

DATHENUS: My dear Elizabeth, be continually commended to God and the Word of His grace (Acts 20:32); and keep diligently that which is entrusted to you (1 Tim. 6:20).

ELIZABETH: Farewell also, my dear friend. The Lord will richly reward you for these efforts. When I get home, I will joyfully sing the Song of Mary and will rejoice in the God of my salvation (Ps. 35:9; Luke 1:46-55), always and forever (Phil. 4:4). Amen.

Finis. June 24, 1584; [sent] to Ghent.